What Smart Couples Know: The Secret to a Happy Relationship

Patricia Covalt, Ph.D.

AMACOM

American Management Association

New York • Atlanta • Brussels • Chicago • Mexico City • San Francisco
Shanghai • Tokyo • Toronto • Washington, D.C.

Special discounts on bulk quantities of AMACOM books are available to corporations, professional associations, and other organizations. For details, contact Special Sales Department, AMACOM, a division of American Management Association, 1601 Broadway, New York, NY 10019.
Tel.: 212-903-8316. Fax: 212-903-8083.
Web Site: www.amacombooks.org

This publication is designed to provide accurate and authoritative information in regard to the subject matter covered. It is sold with the understanding that the publisher is not engaged in rendering legal, accounting, or other professional service. If legal advice or other expert assistance is required, the services of a competent professional person should be sought.

Library of Congress Cataloging-in-Publication Data

Covalt, Patricia
  What smart couples know: the secret to a happy relationship/Patricia Covalt
      p. cm.
    Includes bibliographical references and index.
    ISBN-13: 978-0-8144-0921-3
    ISBN-10: 0-8144-0921-0
  1. Marriage. 2. Emotional intelligence. I. Title.

HQ734.C86575 2007
158.2'4—dc22   2007002595

Printing number
10 9 8 7 6 5 4 3 2 1

To my parents, the late Fred and Leola Meter:

They contributed to this book by making my existence possible and by instilling the values of persistence, resilience, and hard work. Their message of accepting people, avoiding small-mindedness, and determining to never give up your dreams left a lasting and valuable impression. A marriage can be happy and healthy despite seemingly insurmountable odds, as they so artfully demonstrated. Mom and Dad, this one's for you!

**To the two best gifts ever left under the Tree of Life:
my daughters, Brandon and Heather:**

Brandon, whose brilliance lights up the room and the lives of the many whom she so skillfully touches has taught me the joy of love, the importance of inclusiveness and respect for all humankind, and disdain for exclusiveness, bigotry, and elitism. She has supported me through this long and arduous process, while simultaneously completing her own. Such a Superstar!

Heather, the Little Giant, who was given to me by the Universe to help me learn humility, unconditional love, and wisdom, epitomizes the strength and courage it takes to slay life's dragons despite detractors and those who doubt. The depth of her spirituality reflects one of the foundations for this book without which life would have little meaning. One of my best teachers!

CONTENTS

TO SANDI SARVER
Technical/Editorial Consultant

I am greatly indebted to Sandi for her undying loyalty to the completion of this book. She applies her positive energy and many gifts to the challenge of helping aspiring authors achieve their goals. To this book, Sandi contributed endless hours of collaboration, consultation, research, application of computer technology skills, editing, and advising. She also provided inspiration, coaching, encouragement, optimism, and creativity. I have learned that one cannot publish a book without such assistance. I would recommend anyone desirous of publishing a book to seek her out. Thanks a million, Sandy.

ACKNOWLEDGMENTS

There are many whom I wish to recognize and who deserve this expression of my deep gratitude.

Jacquie Flynn, Executive Editor of AMACOM Books, for taking the risk to see the potential in this project. You opened the door to a new growth opportunity and career adventure for me.

My siblings, Lois, Gene, Irene, Bertie, Donna, Phyllis, and Sandra. Completing this project required that I believe in myself. You gave me that belief and perhaps without knowing it, you gave me a vision. You accepted me, loved me, and imparted the outrageous idea that we can do whatever we set our minds to. God bless you all for that.

My friends and colleagues for your loyalty and undying faith in my ability to complete this project. Though I was neglectful at times, thank you for being steadfast in doing what friends do: LaMese Hurrell-Coupe, Rhoda Guerin, Susan Baker, Dr. Sandra McIntire, Karen Sandvold, Jill Cackowski, Dr. Claire Karam, Brenda Carmody, Dr. Hale Martin, and countless others whom I am privileged to call "friend."

Grover, my very gifted partner, my companion. You provided the safe harbor for the birthing and completion of this book. You reinforced my belief that we are obliged to use our God-given talents and to give back from what we have been given. Your support has made it possible for me to keep my eye on that star in the distance.

My clients, for contributing to nearly thirty years of daily transformation as we collaborated on a journey of growth, healing, and learning. You have given me the opportunity to be a vessel in the career I truly love. This book is unquestionably about and for *you*.

The Pastoral Care Team and my friends at Unity Church of Denver who persisted in providing inspiration and the reassurance that comes with the power of prayer.

New friends and acquaintances at Lockheed Martin Corporation, for your interest in the unfolding of this book and your support along the way.

IMPORTANT DISCLAIMER

This book contains my opinions and ideas for the purpose of providing helpful information on the topics presented herein. Neither I, as author, nor the publisher are offering medical services through this content. You are advised to consult medical or other professionals before attempting to apply any of the suggestions or guidelines provided in this book.

The publisher and I disclaim all responsibility for any liability, loss, or risk, which is incurred as a result of the use or application of any of the subject matter in this publication.

INTRODUCTION

Everyone who reads my book will find it helpful and applicable to their lives. It provides a unique formula for committed relationships which we all have had, are involved in, or are desirous of. The unique formula I refer to is the power and importance of emotional intelligence in our personal lives and relationships. Without EQ we cannot relate effectively.

When I first learned of the concept of emotional intelligence and became aware it was applied extensively in the academic and business worlds, it seemed incredulous to me that so few had seen the wisdom of applying these aptitudes in committed relationships or marriage. I began to search for resources that made this important connection and ultimately decided to do it myself. Numerous publications exist which indirectly address certain aspects of emotional intelligence, but very few relate exclusively to EQ in love relationships or marriage.

As I have observed the struggles of countless individual clients and couples in my clinical work over twenty-seven years, I cannot help but want to stop the pain and ease the struggle. Likewise, as I witness the potential for joy, it becomes essential to call attention to the personal development made possible through awareness and improvement in EQ which ushers in this satisfaction. While most people want to create satisfying marriages or love relationships, many of us are baffled by why it is so difficult or so often does not really meet our needs. There are thousands of books available on the topics of marriage and relationships, but this book provides something special. It focuses a great deal on us as individuals in these dyads and is one of the first to offer a link between this widely heralded theory of emotional intelligence and our most important interactions.

We all encounter individuals in public and social settings who expound upon love and marriage with great enthusiasm and a sense of authority—

whether it is a family member at dinner, a companion at the bar, or a co-worker. However, these issues are far more complex than the average "expert" believes them to be. Both marriage and divorce are taken too lightly; and this has far-reaching ramifications for our children, families, communities, and our culture as a whole. What is called for is a much deeper understanding of the qualities which have to be developed in us, the individuals, who comprise our relationship or marriage so they can be fully functional for the good of all concerned.

One of life's greatest blessings is being able to do the work you love. What could be better than following your passion and making a career of it? And so it is with my clinical work and the birthing of this book. Entering the private, intimate lives of individuals, couples, and families for over a quarter of a century with the intent of facilitating healthy functioning is both humbling and enormously enriching.

During the time I have provided psychotherapy to these populations, I have also conducted the well-known and widely used divorce recovery workshop Rebuilding: When Your Relationship Ends originated by the late Dr. Bruce Fisher. Witnessing the devastation of divorce in the lives of thousands of families is strong motivation to help keep marriages intact. I am not a marriage counselor but a psychotherapist specializing in several areas of mental health, one of which is committed love relationships, including marriage.

Readers who welcome uplifting resources will find that my book offers hope and optimism. It is based in part on Positive Psychology, a relatively new field in the science of Psychology. Among many other relevant topics, it also includes a focus on two issues of current popular interest and how they apply to our relationships: the mind-body connection and a down to earth discussion of mature spirituali.

PART I

CHAPTER ONE

Laying the Foundation

Maturity is a time when we stop hiding our
strengths from ourselves out of fear and begin to
live at our best level—instead of below it.

—UN SECRETARY GENERAL DAG HAMMARSKJÖLD

"I love her as a person, of course, but I'm not 'in love' with her anymore."

"I have tried everything—reading, workshops, therapy—you name it! And I still fail at love relationships! What is wrong with me?"

"Mary and I have been married for twenty-five years and have worked hard on our relationship, but I'm still not happy . . . "

"My divorce was so painful; I just know I'll never find the right person for me."

"Jan is so cold anymore. We used to have a lot of fun, but our sex life is like a desert now. Maybe I should look elsewhere."

"I have dated dozens of available men and done everything the experts suggest. But I can't find a man who measures up to my standards. The best guys are already taken."

"Ever since the children came, we are like two ships passing in the night. She has her life; I have mine. I'd like to be in a happy marriage again."

"He has hurt me too many times. I would be a fool to forgive him and stay in this relationship, but I can't seem to leave it."

"My parents weren't particularly happy or well suited. Nor were my grandparents. But they stayed together. I don't expect to be fulfilled or happy in my marriage. We just get by, year after year."

"I had reservations about marrying her on the day of our wedding. I find myself looking at other women. I should never have gotten myself into this."

"We just don't meet each other's needs. I think it's a myth that people can really be happily married. I don't know of anyone who is."

Resonate with any of these quotes? Or something close to them? Would you like to be able to create a lasting healthy relationship? You can. Apply what you learn in this book about *emotional intelligence* (EQ) and be guaranteed greater success and satisfaction. Guaranteed? Yes. You'll learn something new and perhaps change your attitude, feelings, and behavior—but it's worth it. This works!! *Emotional intelligence* may be something you have never heard about or given much consideration to.

Turn on your TV in the morning and flip through the channels. Do the same in the afternoon and again in the evening. Do this for several days and notice how much attention is given to adult love relationships: shows extolling the virtues and bliss of "true love" and romance; talk shows dramatizing the perils, pitfalls, and pain; interviews or in-depth conversations with experts or those claiming to be experts who have all the answers to your relationship woes; promises that you will live happily ever after if you participate in their programs.

Observe the newsstand in your favorite market. You will see rows of books and magazines bombarding you with the same thing. If we have so much information available to us, why do we continue to have so many problems with our relationships? And why is the divorce rate so high?

Is there a magic wand? Well, sort of. Some of the books, shows, and programs you see advertised are right on target, but you need EQ to make them work! If the book you read or the program/workshop in which you participate is about communication, you must have EQ to apply what you learn. The same is true for managing conflict. The same is true for improving your sexual relations. The same is true when dealing with infidelity. The same is true for recovering from divorce and starting over. EQ—the magic wand!

The good news is that you already have a certain level of EQ. Use it. Improve it. Build on it. Be consistent. It will greatly enhance your relationships. Of course, it would be best if your partner did the same.

Some people just want a relationship—any relationship. They want to be part of a couple and do not care about the quality. But what if you want a healthy, lasting, and fulfilling relationship? Then you'll need EQ, and this book is for you.

Relationship success is dependent both on what you *do* as well as on who you *are.* Therapy and self-help resources are often designed to help you develop specific necessary skills, but successful relationships require more than just skill!

Unfortunately many people focus more on finding the right person than on being the right person.

Clearly, while none of us is an island, we are all individuals. You probably want to be the best person you can be for your partner, right? And you want him/her to be his/her best for you. OK. That is possible.

Think about this:

- Would your relationship run more smoothly if you sharpened your ability to read and understand your partner's feelings?

- Would you both feel better if you could show your partner that you're "tuned in" to him/her?

- If the two of you had more positive than negative interactions and were more optimistic about the relationship, would things improve?

- Would it improve things for the two of you if you read your partner's "signals" more accurately and he/she did the same for you?

- Would things be better if you could both clearly identify and then appropriately express your own emotions?

- Would things change for the better if the two of you showed more empathy and compassion for each other?

- And what about the hard times? If you could both hang in there and be persistent or enthusiastic in solving problems or facing setbacks, would that make things easier?

- Would it feel better if you admired and valued each other more?

If you're tempted to respond, "Well, duh. Of course, everyone would want these things in their relationships," be assured that you can have things this way by using your EQ. If you are frustrated with your relationships, use your EQ more and improve upon it. This book helps you do that.

I recently sat down with a couple on the brink of divorce. She is hurt and angry. He is hurt and angry. She blames him. He blames her. He doesn't hear what she is saying. She doesn't hear what he is saying. There is no compassion or empathy for each other. They barely know how to handle themselves, let alone each other. Fortunately, they are motivated to save the marriage, open to learning, and willing to change. A transfusion of EQ into their relationship could help them save it.

Now let's look at a success story. This couple has dated for four years and been engaged for more than a year. They too were angry, hurt, and blaming when I first met with them. She had grown up with an alcoholic mother, and he an alcoholic father. He had a pattern of being controlling and angry, and she was critical and withdrawing. Both would get "fed up" when problems came up and not want to work things out. Slowly they have come to know themselves better and see themselves more realistically. Currently, they are each "looking in the mirror" to see how they make things worse when they let their emotions run rampant and are not tuned in to each other. He has become less impulsive. She has become more compassionate. They are seeing each other and their relationship more positively and are feeling more empowered. And both are persisting, despite the hard work it requires. In short, they are both developing more EQ and using it! All the communication workshops, conflict management classes, and marriage enrichment programs in the world would not help them without their use of EQ.

And so it goes—year after year, couple after couple. People willing to take the journey—seeing what they are capable of and what is possible for them to accomplish together. It is revolutionary.

I wrote this book with a deep passion to help you be more successful in your relationships. If you are married,

Some studies show that more educated couples tend to be happier than those less educated, but I find that the presence of EQ is an even more influential factor than education or socioeconomic status.

you and your partner can take this journey together. If you both use your EQ, you'll be amazed at what can happen. If you are single, it will give you hope for a successful future relationship.

There are a number of structured training programs available to help you develop or increase EQ as it relates to your work or academic life. But there are very few such training programs for developing or increasing your EQ for your personal life and relationships. Specific techniques and exercises are provided in this book for that purpose. Think of this book as your own "personal trainer" to get your EQ in shape.

Are you skeptical that the two of you can make the changes? Have hope. Your attitudes, behaviors, and emotions can change. Fortunately, the human brain is in a constant learning mode. Try to avoid "copping out" with the excuse that "this is just who I am and I can't change" or giving up on your partner with the claim that "he/she will never change."

The first two questions I ask couples in marital therapy are listed below. How would you answer these questions?

- How much do you want this relationship to continue? (i.e., How strong is your commitment?)

- Are you willing to learn, do the work, and make the changes that are necessary to improve it?

Have you focused your attention on your partner's flaws or how he/she upsets you rather than on yourself? This book helps you concentrate on how your own EQ can help you change and save, strengthen, or establish a relationship. You are more likely to *succeed*, of course, if you are *both* working at the EQ training program.

In the not too distant past we were faced with social pressures, cultural expectations, and social mores that kept us in our marriages. Most people stayed married if they fulfilled their prescribed role as husband or wife. This is no longer the case. With these pressures and expectations fading, it is the emotional and psychological forces in our lives that play the key role in our marriages. It is no longer enough to just fulfill socially prescribed roles.

Today it is these emotional ties that are supposed to be the glue that keeps us together. Most of us expect personal closeness, meaningful and effective communication, companionship, intimacy, good sex, support, and equality. But we need to be skilled and intelligent in these areas if we are to get all of these things from our relationship.

It is of the utmost importance that both you and your partner understand the value of EQ for optimal functioning and relating.

Both men and women benefit from relationships in certain ways. Men are less likely than women to make their marriage their primary source of happiness, although this is changing. They are more inclined to look to outside activities and their careers for fulfillment. In contrast, even though the majority of women are working in careers outside the home, they are more likely to get their relational needs met through fulfilling relationships with friends and family than they are at work. In general, women are more likely than men to be aware of their needs for personal and emotional connections; men are not always effective in meeting their own psychological needs or those of their female partners.

You may know that "something is wrong" with your relationship. Or you claim that "we don't communicate very well," "we fight all the time," "we just don't understand each other," or "we are *The field of EQ is a virtual gold mine as it relates to adult love interactions.* so different than each other." The chapters that follow will give you the confidence and ability you need to unravel and change these common dilemmas.

A WORD ABOUT DIVORCE

Clearly divorce is a painful experience for everyone involved, and for many of us, it is the most difficult experience of our lifetimes thus far. To minimize the effect of this trauma on our families, ourselves, and society is a grave mistake. While some of us fare better than others, divorce ravages the lives of millions every day. It is in some way traumatic in nearly every case.

Those most harmed by divorce are, of course, the children. Sixty percent of all two-year-olds will end up in a single-parent family before age eighteen. Our divorce rate of 50% is staggering and needs to be taken seriously. It is a myth that our children are so resilient that they just "bounce back" naturally and that we needn't worry about their adjustment. The facts clearly do not support this. The trauma of divorce is often carried into our adult years in significantly harmful ways.

The best way to minimize the traumatic effects of divorce on our children is for us, the parents, to maintain cordial and cooperative interactions with *Do you want to avoid divorce? Then develop your EQ!* each other during and after the divorce. And without question, this requires EQ! Obviously divorce is something that should be prevented. Learning all you can about how to build and maintain a healthy relationship is worth the effort it may take. It takes two people to make a relationship work but only one to get a divorce.

Fortunately, there is a trend toward first marriages occurring later in life, with greater numbers of us marrying in our thirties and forties. This trend is encouraging. We all know of couples who married quite young and had a happy, healthy life together. But there are a number of advantages to marrying later, and in most cases, with some unfortunate exceptions, people mature as they get older.

Generally speaking, if you postpone your first marriage, you are more likely to work out personal issues and experience things you need to get behind you before committing to the serious institution of marriage: complete your education, establish a career, have more clarity on what is best for you, and be more emotionally mature. Hopefully this trend will play a role in reducing the rate and the devastating impact of divorce. But age alone will not make you more emotionally intelligent or guarantee that you will live "happily ever after."

A Bit of History: Origins of the Concept of Emotional Intelligence

Emotional intelligence is a topic of both popular interest and serious research. This book is primarily for those of you who are more interested in popular psychology and self-help/personal growth.

Yale psychologist, Peter Salovey, Ph.D., mapped the ways in which we can bring intelligence to our emotions and provided a framework for the interaction between emotions and reasoning.

In a groundbreaking article published in 1990 with John D. Mayer, Ph.D., Peter Salovey, Ph.D., defined EQ as "the subset of social intelligence that involves the ability to monitor one's own and the other's feelings and emotions, to discriminate among them, and to use this information to guide one's thinking."[1]

In essence, this means having the capacity to understand your emotions and the emotions of others and to use reason in handling this emotional information. This in turn guides our behavior as well. Mayer and Salovey's work helped to shift from the traditional view of emotion as haphazard and immature to the current, more positive view of emotion as adaptive and useful for organizing and guiding our thoughts and actions.

We can and should use our emotions as a resource to solve the problems in our lives. If you are more capable of good personal communication, empathy, and connection with others, you are less likely to be depressed.

While we are all different in our processing styles and abilities, EQ and its accompanying skills can be learned or improved, and this contributes to our overall mental health and our relationships.

The field of general intelligence adds credibility to the notion of EQ. Eminent psychologist E. L. Thorndike, Ph.D., contributed significantly in the 1920s and 1930s to our modern understanding of intelligence quotient (IQ) and the use of IQ testing. It is noteworthy that he proposed that social intelligence, a subset of EQ, reflects an aspect of our general IQ. He defined social intelligence as having the ability to perceive our own and others' internal states, motives, and behaviors; to act toward them optimally on the basis of that information; and to relate to people effectively.

Also noteworthy is that David Wechsler, Ph.D., the author of the most widely used tests for measuring individual intelligence, called intelligence "the aggregate or global capacity of the individual to act purposefully, think rationally, and deal effectively with one's environment."[2] Wechsler says that intelligence is not only cognitive processes or academic performance and skills, but it also includes how we interact with others, manage our behavior and emotions, and function in life in general.

The individual whose work has had the most powerful impact on my views on EQ is science journalist Daniel Goleman, Ph.D. His best seller, *Emotional Intelligence: Why It Can Matter More Than IQ,* popularized this concept.

Goleman's work is widely applicable to business and industry, and his theories are used in academic settings throughout the world. He has helped thousands to see that emotions play a crucial role in their everyday lives and that most of us can be more emotionally competent. I found his book to be quite relevant to close personal relationships.

While it is true that the amount of control you have over your emotional responses has a genetic component, you can still learn to manage your emotions to a certain degree. Most of us do learn this at some point. This means that EQ is learnable.

I recently attended a management organization dinner during which the keynote speaker, a top executive in the aeronautics industry, made a call for the necessity of increased EQ in his industry. This example demonstrates that even in the most scientific industries or communities the qualities of EQ are essential for optimal personal functioning and relating to others.

NINE COMPONENTS OF EMOTIONAL INTELLIGENCE

There are a number of abilities or aptitudes of the emotionally intelligent person.[3] I have chosen the nine listed below because they are necessary to your love relationship. They are presented in an order that may represent their importance. Each one of these EQ skills and abilities is distinct and separate; but there is significant interaction among them, with one depending on or building upon another.

1. Being self-aware and having self-knowledge

2. Knowing, understanding, regulating or managing your emotions, and expressing or using them appropriately and adaptively

3. Empathizing and being attuned to others, especially your partner, and dealing with them effectively

4. Maintaining hope, positive thinking, and an attitude of optimism

5. Keeping distress from swamping your ability to think—being able to override negative emotions or moods to be able to think and function appropriately

6. Maintaining enthusiasm and persistence in the face of frustration or setbacks and having the capacity to tolerate defeat

7. Maintaining a sense of self-efficacy

8. Delaying gratification and controlling or resisting your impulses, both emotionally and in actions

9. Being self-motivated—managing your emotions to reach a goal

In essence, if you are an emotionally intelligent individual, you are likely to be more mentally healthy, create a fulfilling life for yourself, and be comfotable to be around because you contribute to the well-being of others. Conversely, if you lack these qualities, you are more likely to become a slave to your emotions, have less satisfying relationships, be less likely to create a life that fulfills you emotionally, and possibly be insensitive or hurtful to others.

Let's look at some examples:

Self-Awareness

At thirty-seven, Greg is ready to establish a lasting relationship and get married. After his last "heartbreak" when the woman he was dating ended their relationship, he began to carefully examine who he was and what had gone wrong in his relationships.

He looked at his early life and what influenced his choices and ways of relating. He observed his behavior and got feedback from friends and family. He journaled, read books, and even asked the woman who had left him to give him feedback. He was getting to know and understand himself better and is ready to make changes—an essential first step.

Empathy, Attunement, and Self-Efficacy

Hanna has suffered from depression and physical health issues for most of her life. John, her husband of twenty-five years, is an upbeat person with a good sense of humor, but he often used it to discount her feelings. While she suffered, he laughed and made jokes, sometimes ridiculing her and sometimes trying to "cheer her up."

His lack of empathy and compassion just made things worse. Now she is learning to take charge of her pain, is becoming more empowered (self-efficacy), and is feeling better. John is now able to respond to his wife with sincere empathy (attunement). The outcome for them is hopeful.

Managing Emotions

Rhonda cried at the drop of a hat, so to speak, and also became instantly angry when things did not go her way. She alienated friends, created chasms between herself and her husband, and upset her children.

She is learning that she has developed poor emotional habits, which began in her childhood. She is learning to tune in to herself, including her body, when she is upset; to stop and breathe; to center herself; to identify and change thoughts and feelings; and to make different choices about how she reacts.

Her marriage is improving and the family is running more smoothly. New habits can replace old ones.

Maintaining Hope and Optimism

Andy cheated on Zoe, and a child resulted from his affair. At first Zoe felt that her world had collapsed. They had one older child, and she thought their marriage had been going well. She was furious and humiliated; Andy was ashamed and remorseful. They fought, cried, and discussed it endlessly.

Then they settled in and decided to try to save their marriage. At times it felt hopeless, but they were determined to be optimistic. They have struggled to be positive about each other and the future. And it's working.

Each of these vignettes leaves out important details to protect the identity of the individuals described, but they demonstrate actual applications of EQ in relationships.

MATURITY

As you proceed through this book, it will become clear that the more mature you are, the more likely you are to possess EQ or be willing and able to develop your EQ qualities. Most of our relationships/marriages consist of two wounded children in grown-up bodies. To create a truly satisfying relationship, each of us must make every effort to think, feel, and act in as mature a way as possible.

Some components of maturity include:

- Handling frustration and settling differences in nondestructive ways

- Being patient, civil, and kind

- Having a willingness to postpone gratification

- Using perseverance in the face of setbacks

- Taking ownership or accountability for your actions, attitudes, and feelings

- Facing unpleasantness without bitterness

- Displaying humility and the ability to say, "I'm sorry" or "I was wrong"

- Accepting responsibility for the outcome of your decisions

- Being dependable

- Maintaining personal integrity

- Avoiding judgmental and critical attitudes toward others

- Having a general acceptance of others and an attitude of inclusiveness

Imagine the success rate of marriages if more of us possessed the nine EQ qualities and operated from a place of maturity! Wow! Revolutionary!

POSITIVE PSYCHOLOGY

You may be tempted to "overpathologize" or focus on what is wrong with you instead of building on your strengths and what is right. If you are someone who has experienced a great deal of pain and woundedness throughout your life, you may need to first focus on fixing what is wrong and work on healing. But in doing this, try to emphasize your strengths and potential. This will definitely pay dividends for both you and your partner.

It is a mistake to deny or overlook any deep psychological, physical, social, or spiritual pain that results from trauma or from emotional and mental illness. But your personal growth or healing can be as focused on strength, resilience, and wellness as it is on weakness, vulnerability, and sickness.

You will find that this book gives you hope and optimism. It has been strongly influenced by the field of positive psychology.

The field of positive psychology is a key motivating force behind this book.

In the millennial (January 2000) issue of the *American Psychologist* the authors of sixteen articles on positive psychology called for a greater emphasis on what leads to psychological well-being and thriving (what is right with us) and less emphasis on pathology (what is wrong with us). We can thrive (not just survive) even under the worst of circumstances.

Positive psychology concerns itself with such issues as those on the following page. Use this as a checklist and ask yourself in which of these areas you are strong and on which you need to work.

- ☐ Well-being
- ☐ Contentment
- ☐ Satisfaction
- ☐ Hope and optimism
- ☐ Flow and happiness
- ☐ Courage
- ☐ Capacity for love and vocation
- ☐ Perseverance
- ☐ Forgiveness

- ☐ Originality
- ☐ Future mindedness
- ☐ Spirituality
- ☐ High Talent
- ☐ Wisdom
- ☐ Responsibility
- ☐ Nurturing
- ☐ Altruism
- ☐ Civility
- ☐ Moderation
- ☐ Tolerance

- ☐ Self-direction
- ☐ Maturity
- ☐ Work ethic
- ☐ Autonomy
- ☐ Intrinsic motivation
- ☐ Interpersonal skills
- ☐ Self-determination
- ☐ Creativity
- ☐ Humor

Can you see the overlap between this positivistic view and what it means to be emotionally intelligent?

In recent years there has been a shift in the field of medicine from a predominant focus on disease and illness to a more prevention-focused perspective. In the past psychology and psychiatry did not give much attention to positive transformations and were too focused on pathology. But research shows that most of our struggles can be buffered, relieved, and in some cases prevented by certain positive strengths such as those listed above. For example, there is significant evidence that positivism and optimism serve to prevent and alleviate depression in some people.

When it comes to relationships, it is not enough to just help those of us who are miserable or on the brink of divorce. We all need help in maintaining or achieving more fulfilling lives. Considerable scientific information is available about the neurology and chemistry of severe mental illness, substance abuse, anxiety, and depression, but little is known about the neurochemistry and anatomy of our positive qualities and experiences.

If we expect the outcomes in our lives to be positive, it is more likely they will be positive.

You can be relatively happy while confronting life and its many problems realistically. As human beings, we are naturally drawn to happiness, well-being, and optimism. Optimism can lead to good moods, perseverance, achievement, physical health, effective problem solving, and success in life. It is not a coincidence that an attitude of optimism is woven throughout this book.

In general, we adapt and return to a positive attitude even after we have experienced a tragedy or loss. We reframe such questions as: Is my life good or bad? Are people in general good or bad? Is my partner basically a good person or not? And is our relationship a disaster or do we just need to make it better?

SUMMARY

Have fun as you proceed through this book and notice how the reading, checklists, and inventories will help you improve your EQ. Chapters 9 through 15 are specifically devoted to providing detailed exercises and techniques which, if you apply them, will make you say, "Yes! I can make my relationship better."

While some inventories measure EQ in the workplace and in schools, no comprehensive statistically based instrument is available for scientifically measuring EQ in love relationships at this time. However, the self-tests and checklists in this book will help you understand your own level of EQ, how you might improve it, and how it can be applied to your relationship/marriage.

Consider that there are far-reaching society-wide benefits that result from healthy and successful love relationships/marriages. You could be part of that transformation. Enjoy the journey as you become the best partner you can be. Be open, be positive, work at it—be more emotionally intelligent!

CHAPTER TWO

Who Am I?

Beginning the Journey

Inside myself is a place where I live all
alone and that's where you renew your
springs that never dry up.

—PEARL BUCK

Both singles and couples tend to focus on people other than themselves. If you are single, you may give too much attention to "the search" for a partner who is right for you; if you are in a relationship, you are likely to concentrate more on the strengths and weaknesses of your mate than on your own features. Remember that being the right person is much more important than finding or being with the right person.

Relationships are comprised of two separate, individual persons; we must be capable of contributing to appropriate interactions.

Your individual personality and style have great impact on your committed relationship. It is important to look at *who* you are, *how* you became who you are, your behavior, and the effect it has on your interactions with your partner.

This chapter will help you examine how you developed your personality, your style of relating to others, your emotional patterns or habits, the benefits of self-disclosure, and the value of positive thoughts and feelings. It will become clear to you how essential emotional intelligence (EQ) is to all of this.

So what is your personality? You can think of it as your consistent patterns of behavior and the emotions, motivations, and thoughts that guide how you act and feel. The term *consistent* is important here because some aspects of your personality can be identified across time and situations and do not change quickly. Fortunately, other things about your personality can and do change. Sometimes this takes conscious effort and sometimes not. It can also be affected by your interactions with others. If you are interested in assessing your personality or understanding your style, there are numerous tools for doing this.

A certain amount of EQ may be present in your personality as it is now, but this can be further developed. You can increase your self-awareness and come to understand yourself better; learn to regulate and manage your emotions, expressing them more appropriately; and replace a negative outlook on life with a more optimistic one—all of which are addressed in this chapter. To some degree, you can make these changes on your own, but you will also need feedback and interaction with others. The exercises outlined in Part III (Chapters 8 through 15) will help with this.

There are a number of theories and perspectives on how we become the people we are and how we bring certain personality characteristics, habits, styles, and idiosyncrasies into our interactions with others. Each of these is a well-developed school of thought based on years of research and application. They help us understand what is called "individual differences." These include: psychoanalytic, trait, biological/physiological, behavioral/social learning, cognitive, neo-Freudian, humanistic, and systems theory. If you are interested in a brief description of each of these, you will find them in Appendix A.

You are not a "finished product" when you reach adulthood. You continue to change and grow throughout your lifetime from birth to old age. Regardless of which viewpoint or theory you use, it is important to keep this in mind as you work to increase your EQ and improve the way you relate to others.

HOW DID I BECOME WHO I AM?

You no doubt have heard of the "nature vs. nurture" debate. Let's take a look at this. Your family of origin and early life experiences play a key role in the development of your personality and thus your adult interactions. This is not said to discount the genetically influenced or natural tendencies that are present in your personality. Most experts claim our personalities are determined approximately 45% to 50% by early life influences and 45% to 50% by genetic heritage and physiology.

Life experiences, your own efforts, or clinical treatment can influence and modify inherited factors to a degree. Certain things about you may be genetically influenced or determined, but that

This book focuses on the influence of "nurture" and less on "nature," or inheritable, genetic factors.

does not mean they are genetically fixed. The more changeable aspects of your personality and the way you function are those on the nurture side of the "nature vs. nurture" question. These are the things that came from your life experiences and the patterning of others.

As we grow to understand ourselves, it is important that we live in the now, the present, and avoid focusing too much on the past or the future. However, many of us cannot do this because either the wounds from our earlier experiences must first be healed or the influences of the past have been so strong that we need to face and deal with them first. Your ultimate goal should be to live fully in the present, but it may be tough to do this without working through your past.

Goleman says that early emotional hardships and trauma have an enduring and pervasive effect on adulthood and that psychotherapy may be required for some individuals to change these patterns.

We sometimes explain our problems, inappropriate behavior patterns, or personality characteristics with, "It is common in my family" or "I have a chemical imbalance as others do in my family." Obviously, you should consider your genetic history to understand your personality or a mental health condition. However, be careful not to overuse this to explain who you are. It can be as much of a "copout" as being stuck in blaming your life experiences. Self-efficacy, or a belief in your ability to manage the outcomes of your life, takes you out of the "victim" role. You are neither a victim of your genetics nor of your life experiences.

The functioning of your brain, nervous system, and physiology that contribute to your personality are hugely affected by your life experiences and vice versa. The more you understand yourself, the more likely you are to take charge of your life in a positive way, despite your own biology.

Let's take a look at the effects of your life experiences. Below are some examples of situations that can have negative effects on personality formation and development. Examine this list and identify any that you experienced in your early life.

- Alcoholism of one or both parents

- Physical, emotional, or sexual abuse

- Emotional or physical neglect

- Death of a parent

- Emotional or mental illness of one or both parents

- Role reversals and "parentification" of a child

- Overindulgence

- Unclear limits or boundaries

- Rigid, overcontrolling, or excessively strict atmosphere

- Lack of love and affection

If you had secure, stable, loving parents in a safe, appropriate environment, this is likely to have had a positive effect on your personality formation. Either way, this early experience contributed to your current level of EQ and now influences your adult relationships.

According to neuroscientists, your memories are stored in your brain as early as preverbal infancy (and some say intrauterine), which leads to the feelings you express and the actions you take now. Goleman says, " . . . the interactions of life's earliest years lays down a set of emotional lessons based on the attunement and upsets in the contacts between infant and caretakers . . . One reason we can be so baffled by our emotional outbursts as adults is that they often date from a time early in our lives . . . "[4]

In other words, your memories of experiences, messages, and influences are stored in certain brain centers, and they influence your current feelings and behavior. This is illustrated throughout this book in the examples from people's lives.

If you understand yourself and how you arrived at who you are, you will be able to relate to the notion of your "inner child" much more easily than someone who does not. For a lot of adults, knowing and relating appropriately to their "inner child" can relieve their suffering and free them to become who they want to be.

Much of what you experience throughout your life stays in your unconscious. Research shows that the power of your unconscious plays a major role in forming your personality and influencing your feelings and behaviors.

Swiss psychiatrist and neo-Freudian, Carl Jung, M.D., world renowned for his contributions to the field of psychology from the 1920s through the 1950s, introduced the notion that we choose our marriage partners unconsciously. "The greater the area of unconsciousness, the less is marriage a matter of free choice, as is shown subjectively in the fatal compulsion one feels so acutely when one is in love." Further, "It is the strength (and nature) of the bond to the parents that unconsciously influences the choice of husband or wife, either positively or negatively . . . children are unconsciously driven in a direction that is intended to compensate for everything that was felt unfulfilled in the lives of their parents."[5] If you are grounded in a positive relationship with your parents, you are more likely to adjust to your mate than if you are hindered by an unhealed unconscious tie to them.

In some ways, the couple described here represents a good example of Jung's theory:

Pete and Dana were married for nearly 25 years and clearly brought unfinished and destructive business from their parents into their marriage. Dana, a vital and active woman now in her early 60s, continued to suffer from a "mother wound." Although she had experienced some healing and resolution, she continued to be haunted by her mother, who was rigid, controlling, unaffectionate, insecure, and image conscious, and who doted on her sister while neglecting Dana. Her father was a passive person who deferred to her mother and was absent a great deal. Dana struggled with low self-esteem and a particular lack of confidence in her intellectual abilities. She came to see that she had unconsciously chosen Pete as a marriage partner because he was very much like her mother. She developed a dependent and codependent relationship with him and spent many years trying to please him to no avail.

Pete was raised by a cold, critical, self-absorbed, alcoholic father who openly mistreated his mother and showed little respect for women. Although Pete disliked his father and did not wish to emulate him, he did precisely that. He was self-absorbed in his marriage and eventually became quite cold to and critical of Dana.

Dana entered a "semi-retired" mode, but Pete continued to work because his identity was largely based on his career. As he too faced the possibility of retirement, he began to pull away from Dana and became involved with another woman, and the marriage began to deteriorate. A casual observer would say that he was just experiencing a "midlife crisis" or had the "retirement jitters." Neither of those situations was the case. It was clearly a case of Dana buckling under Pete's style of relating to her, which was a replication of his father's personality and values and of her mother's style as well. This couple eventually divorced.

Dana experienced a lengthy and painful recovery but was highly motivated to establish, perhaps for the first time in her life, a strong sense of self. She became increasingly self-aware, motivated, and enthusiastic, returning to college and developing an attitude of hope and optimism for her future. I am unaware of Pete's progress, as he moved out of state.

Your parents' relationship also has a potentially powerful effect on your own adult interactions. Make sure you fully understand your parents' marriage and your prospective mate's parents' marriage(s) before you marry.

Do you find yourself resisting the idea of examining the influences of your family of origin out of fear of "blaming your parents" because, after all, they "did the best they could"? This is not about blaming or fault finding. It is a detective sleuthing process or excavation to find answers to the question, "How did I become who I am today?" You can learn to manage your emotions and behaviors no matter what situations you encountered while growing up!

Look realistically at the resemblance and relationship between you and your caretakers, the relationship between your caretakers, the relationships between you and your siblings, and any other family factors or incidents that had an impact on you. It is OK to recall both negative and positive qualities of your parents or other caretakers and aspects of your family and early life. You are simply looking at the facts of your upbringing and how they have affected your personality and relating style today.

With proper guidance, we ultimately do not lose respect for or stop loving our parents, other caregivers, or siblings as we examine our early life experiences.

In doing this, you may either notice positive influences you have overlooked or recall the negative and experience some anger or hurt. Positive early life experiences are essential for good mental health, EQ, and proper adult behavior. Seek to understand those things that weren't so great and need healing or attention. Just as a dentist is more focused on your damaged or decaying teeth than on the healthy ones, you may need to focus on your "bruises" or bad memories to move forward.

An example illustrates the impact of early life experience:

Bob is a semi-retired man in his mid-50s. He had never sought professional help and came into therapy at the urging of Hanna, his wife. Bob was very defensive and closed as we began the process, presenting with very little self-awareness or EQ. Hanna complained that he was angry a great deal of the time and emotionally unapproachable. He was also possessive and jealous of her because she was involved in church and other volunteer activities and did not depend on him to fulfill all her needs. In contrast, Bob did not maintain a full life and expected Hanna to be a primary source of entertainment, companionship, and meaning. Bob experienced a major transformation when he began to open up and disclose in therapy his early life experiences. The presence of his paternal grandmother in the family home was an extremely destructive influence in his childhood. Bob's grandmother moved in with them when Bob's grandfather died. Bob was a very small child at the time, and this arrangement continued for nearly thirty years. Grandma never recovered from the loss of her husband, and she lived with Bob's family as a bitter, angry, controlling woman. She was grumpy and mean spirited and the entire family "walked on eggshells." Bob feared her a great deal and observed that there was no closeness allowed among the other family members because they were all constantly in "survival mode." Bob's parents were basically slaves to Grandma, catering to her every need, and had little time to meet each other's needs or the needs of their four children. While no one recognized this at the time, it is highly likely that Grandma suffered from a severe depressive disorder that went untreated.

As our process unfolded, Bob realized that he had never discussed this experience and his resulting pain with anyone, not even Hanna. He had always believed it was disrespectful and inappropriate to identify and talk about ways in which he was hurt and adversely affected by his "elders," including his parents. He began to see that his anger and possessiveness, as well as his inability to fulfill his own needs, came from this early life experience in the family. Bob experienced great relief in "unloading this burden" and was able to progress in the marriage. After many years of living this pattern, it may be some time before he achieves the EQ he desires, but the journey has begun.

ATTACHMENT

Your early attachment style also has a major impact on your marriage and other adult relationships. John Bowlby, M.D., pioneer and leader in the field of attachment theory, helped us understand that the primary motivating principle in human beings is the need to seek and maintain contact with others. His research showed that infants and small children form unconscious models for interpersonal involvement. This means essentially that early experiences with your primary caretakers formed the foundation for the way in which you approach your adult love relationships.

The style of attachment that developed between yourself and your parents in infancy and early childhood influences your emotional expectations in your adult relationships. If your parents were not "in tune" with you as a child, this was likely upsetting to you and may have led to difficulties with a normal exchange of emotions in intimate relationships as an adult. On the other hand, if your parents were very tuned in to you and did a good job of meeting your emotional needs, you are more likely to have healthy emotional exchanges with your adult love partner. Emotionally intelligent parents raise emotionally intelligent kids.

Generally speaking, there are several styles of attachment between parents and children that are carried into adulthood. These general styles are commonly summarized into three categories.

Anxious–ambivalent results from mother/chief caretaker not being adequately attentive or responsive to the needs of the child; the child reacts with more anxiety than is normal when mother/chief caretaker leaves.

Avoidant results when mother/chief caretaker is the same as anxious–ambivalent above, but the child reacts to this by developing a style of detachment or emotional aloofness; the child is not anxious when mother leaves and not desirous of her attention when she returns.

Secure results when mother/chief caretaker is adequately responsive and attentive; the child is generally happy and self-confident and understands that mother is accessible even when not present. It is this latter style, secure, that is ideal for optimal functioning, fulfillment, and happiness.

Susan Johnson, Ed.D., professor of psychology and psychiatry at the University of Ottawa and leader in the field of emotionally focused marital therapy, says that secure attachment occurs when caregivers bond or connect with children in a way that provides a secure base. This results in the individual being capable of developing a view of themselves as lovable and others as reliable and responsive. They are able to trust, view the world as safe, and experience closeness in adult relationships without fear.[6] In other words, if you had a secure attachment to your parents in your earliest years, as an adult you have a greater chance of experiencing this type of secure attachment in marriage. If you did not have this experience in infancy and childhood, chances of achieving this type of attachment in your adult relationships can be greatly enhanced through the use of other appropriate resources.

If you and your partner are able to achieve a "secure attachment" to each other, you are likely to trust each other, be interdependent, support each other, be intimate, be more sensitive, and communicate well. Connection and disconnection or separateness and closeness is negotiated more easily.

If you can achieve and maintain this balance, emotional engagement and responsiveness will be more important than how you resolve your conflicts. I emphasize emotional because this is the key to how well you interact.

Common problems that show up in your relationship/marriage are likely to be the result of threats to secure attachment, either past or present. Inappropriate anger, clinging behavior, jealousy, despair, being controlling, and possessiveness can be triggered when the security of your bond is threatened. Being more emotionally accessible and responsive in your relationship will contribute to a secure attachment.

The research of John Gottman, Ph.D., reveals that emotional disengagement is more predictive of divorce than most other factors and that appropriate emotional engagement is more predictive of successful and satisfying marriages. In some cases, this early emotional bond may be securely in place but broken by such crises as the death of a parent, which can result in difficulty with later adult attachments.

An example of the loss of attachment is helpful:

> Sid represents a classic case of loss of a parent at an early age and the resultant effect on later love relationships. His father was an alcoholic and typically unavailable, but Sid developed a close, secure bond to his mother, whose parenting style was nurturing. Unfortunately, she died of heart failure when he was nine, which was preceded by a lengthy illness. His father did not provide much care to his mother during her illness, a responsibility that Sid took on to some extent. To complicate things further, his father immediately married a woman who was both verbally and physically abusive to Sid and his younger sister.

I worked with Sid individually over a period of several years as well as providing couple therapy to him and his partner. He was a remarkable, high-functioning individual in many ways but continued to exhibit two patterns in these relationships. One was that of the rescuing and caretaking of "damsels in distress"; the other was displaying a clinging, crowding, controlling relationship style. Sid was highly motivated in therapy, improving immeasurably over time in his self-awareness and other aspects of EQ. He was eventually able to work through the early losses and abuse and recognize the resultant relationship patterns. Additionally, Sid chose to return to therapy as needed and participate in other growth-producing activities, which contributed considerably to his ever improving EQ.

Part III (Chapters 8 through 15) provides inventories and self-assessment tools to help you examine and understand your history and how it may have affected you. OK, so what do you do with this information?

SELF-DISCLOSURE

The next step is to share who you are with your partner. Do you have trouble describing your behavior or personality accurately and naming your feelings? Are you able to describe your partner's?

Making a genuine attempt to understand your partner's personality and early experiences requires that you have the ability to tune in to him/her and be empathic as they confide who they are, what they feel, and what they have experienced. Clearly, understanding and sharing yourself with your mate is key to a good relationship/marriage. It is best when each of you reveals information about yourselves at approximately the same level of intimacy.

If you are single and interested in re-entering the world of dating or are searching for a new partner, focus your attention beyond physical attractiveness, how much fun a person is, and your shared interests. Notice or ask questions about another's personality, their history, their life experiences, and how they share their feelings. These are not conversations you rush into upon first meeting, but they are absolutely necessary before you commit to anything serious.

Surprisingly, we may not know much about a committed partner because they have not shared significant life experiences or essential information about their inner experience. There are a number of reasons for this. Check the list below to see if these apply to you:

- You may simply be unable to confide in your partner because you lack the language and awareness to describe yourself and your inner experiences.

- You may be afraid to disclose because you have had painful experiences in sharing with others who betrayed your trust.

- You may have been brought up with the myth that it is unsafe and unwise to "expose your dirty laundry."

- You may feel it is "none of your partner's business." (This is based on fear.)

- You may experience a general discomfort with vulnerability.

- Your partner may show no interest, and so there is little motivation to share.

All of these obstacles, including fear and distrust, can be overcome through increased emotional management on your part and empathy from your partner.

This brief example illustrates the value of self-disclosure:

> Mary and David rushed into marriage after a few months of dating. (I find this to be all too common.) They had not taken the time or had the awareness of the importance of sharing their histories with each other. In social settings and family gatherings David's mother was often very cold and rude to Mary. She would attack David angrily later for not "taking his mother on" to defend her. He was finally able to examine his past experiences and shared tearfully with her that his mother had always been cold, grumpy, and very critical. David became aware that he was still somewhat intimidated by his mother; there was nothing to be gained in confronting her because she remained unapproachable; and it might make things worse. Mary was able to have compassion and empathy for David's feelings and his history with his mother. They were able to agree upon a mutual solution in which David would offer Mary more "behind the scenes" support and empathy during those times when she felt hurt by his mother, and she would not project this hurt onto David angrily.

It is common to deny the effect of what you have been through in the past, and this denial blinds you from seeing the truth. This is made worse by any feelings of shame or the fear of facing the reality of your past or who you truly are. This lack of self-awareness can leave your relationship shallow and unsatisfying.

These examples illustrate the power of denial:

> Several years ago a young, recently divorced single mother disclosed in therapy extensive sexual abuse at the hands of her adoptive father. She then leaned back and with a sigh of relief said, "But I was never sexually abused." It became clear as the therapy process unfolded that while she was genuinely lacking an understanding of what constituted sexual abuse, her level of denial was astonishing. Her shame was so pervasive that she literally could not deal with this trauma. She terminated therapy after dealing with divorce adjustment issues and single parenting and returned several years later, finally ready to move past the denial and face her pain and shame. We proceeded to work on the effects of the sexual abuse, and she was ultimately very grateful she had become ready to do this work.

In another situation a man who came from a family in which both parents were active alcoholics throughout his growing up reported that this "had no effect on him." While this belief and denial are common in the case of alcoholism, you cannot emerge completely unscathed from a home environment in which one or both of your parents were alcoholic. We are not on a "witch hunt" for dysfunction, but don't use denial and delusion when the consequences can be dramatic.

Fortunately, you can learn to establish and maintain healthy adult relationships even though you may have qualities that need to be improved. You do, after all, continue to heal and grow throughout your lifetime if you are self-aware and motivated to be hopeful. You have the power to become who you want to be!

Jung, quoted earlier, encouraged his patients, students, and readers to become acquainted with the "shadow" or dark side of themselves—the hidden, mean, selfish, hurt, inferior base parts of their personalities. You may be afraid to face the embarrassment of exposing your "dirty laundry" or vulnerabilities. And yet who better to do this with than your partner?

Self-disclosure can help you to know yourself. When you are open or transparent with others, you are more likely to be open or transparent to yourself. "Disclosure reciprocity" is a term that means when you disclose personal information to someone, they are more likely to do the same. This usually occurs when you are drawn to another person and can result in mutual trust. It is more likely to happen if you are self-aware, express your emotions appropriately, and are empathic or able to genuinely tune in to others.

Be cautious if you are considering disclosure of extreme trauma. It is best to obtain the guidance of a mental health professional before you discuss trauma with others to avoid triggering or retraumatizing experiences. While it can be healing to verbalize this, in most cases it should first be done with a trusted clinician and then with close friends, loved ones, or your partner.

As you might expect, you benefit most from self-disclosure if someone is listening and responding appropriately. This requires the ability of the listener to truly tune in to the other person who is sharing. Trust can be easily damaged or broken if you disclose personal, sensitive information and your mate does not listen carefully or respond in a caring way.

So how do you begin this process?

In general, the amount of self-disclosure in a marriage is a strong predictor of marital satisfaction.

If there is a mutual willingness and adequate sensitivity, ask simple questions such as those listed below. Use these as a guide for getting your partner to self-disclose. Add to this list using your own judgment of what you consider important to know about him/her. Do this as part of conversations over time, not as an "inquisition" or interview.

About Your Partner's Current Life:

- How would you describe your personality?

- How are you similar to your mother?

- How are you similar to your father?

- What is most important to you in life? Least important?

- Share your thoughts with me about _____.

- Share your feelings with me about _____.

- How do you handle problems such as_____?

- How do you feel about (specific) people in your life?

- What are your religious beliefs? Political beliefs?

- Tell me about your current friendships.

- How well do you feel you know yourself?

- Tell me your views on people in general.

- What are you good at?

- What are your weaknesses?

- Have you taken any personality tests such as the Myers-Briggs?

- What are your fondest memories? Worst memories?

About Your Partner's Early Life:

- Describe your family of origin and the effect they had on you.

- What was it like growing up?

- Tell me about your friendships as a child. As a teen.

- What was your mother like when you were a child?

- What kind of a person was your father when you were a child?

- How did you feel about yourself as a child? As a teen?

- In what activities did you participate?

- What was your neighborhood like?

- What were your church-related experiences, if any?

- Tell me about your siblings and your relationships with them.

- How did your parents relate to each other?

- How did your parents treat you?

- Which of your needs were met when you were a child? Which were not?

- Did you experience any major traumas? Any losses?

- Did you have any great achievements or triumphs?

- What was your father's main message to you about life? About you?

- What was your mother's main message to you about life? About you?

- Share with me any school or educational accomplishments of which you are particularly proud. Any failures?

When you do this with your partner, use genuine interest and do it over time. This exercise is not intended to be done overnight or with overkill.

Ideally you should talk about these things while you are dating and absolutely during an engagement and before marriage. Together you can talk about the impact this has on your relationship or ways you think it might affect you in the future. Most people are not well versed in how to analyze this information and these influences. However, you can ask questions, explore together, and make a concerted effort to get to know yourself and each other better. What is disclosed must not be used against your partner at a later time. Chapter 9 provides a number of suggestions and tools to help you with this.

EMOTIONAL PATTERNS, STYLES, AND HABITS

Some of us develop damaging emotional habits that "show up" in our relationship/marriage as a result of our personality styles and life experiences. These habits or patterns interfere with our EQ and thus with our interactions. What follows is a brief examination of three common examples.

Anger

One of these patterns or habits is being habitually or constantly angry. This might be a bad habit picked up from patterning an angry parent or not learning to deal with life's frustrations, or it may be the result of abuse, early loss, or other trauma. It could also be a symptom of depression. Either way, the constant use of anger is potentially troublesome in your relationship/marriage. It may be a seductive and energizing emotion, and you may feel empowered only when you are angry. You may know of no other way to assert yourself in your relationship or to get your needs met than by using anger.

Angry thoughts clearly fuel angry feelings (and vice versa), which can lead to inappropriate actions.

When your emotions have a life of their own and are not consciously managed, they can wreak havoc in your relationship/marriage. When one of you is constantly or inappropriately angry, this erodes your foundation like "emotional termites." Even in cases of depression most moods, including an angry one, can be managed to some degree. If you are truly emotionally intelligent, you can manage your anger.

You can learn how to reframe potentially volatile issues or situations to diffuse your anger toward a partner. Reframing means looking at something or someone in a fresh and different way, giving a situation or individual the benefit of the doubt. Another powerful way to defuse your anger is to change the convictions or beliefs that are fueling it. As difficult as it may seem, this regulation and management of emotion is possible even when you are angry.

Empathy and compassion, essential to your love relationship and key to emotional intelligence, are absent when you are in an angry state of mind. Common sense tells us that when we are angry and either brooding or lashing out at someone, empathy goes out the window.

If you and your partner are in constant conflict and feeling angry toward one another you do not tune in to each other's feelings and needs. To be able to empathize and really hear what your partner is saying or experiencing requires you to be calm and not blinded by emotion.

An emotionally intelligent person can learn to manage both fear and anger. These emotions do not need to have lives of their own.

Fear

Another emotional pattern that can have a negative impact on your relationship is pervasive fear. Some of us have a general sense of insecurity and do not experience the world as a safe place. This can show up as suspicion, jealousy, defensiveness, possessiveness, an unwillingness to try new activities or endeavors, clinging behaviors, and the like. Habitual fear may also reveal a struggle with your self-esteem or self-confidence, which tends to weigh heavily on a relationship.

Even if you have severe emotional wounds, you can learn to manage your emotions and resultant behaviors.

Some experts claim that fear and anxiety are the core primary emotions underlying our other emotions, that we generally are motivated by fear more than any other emotion, and that we live lives that are, to some degree, "fear based." This may be true, but keep in mind that if your fears become severe or debilitating, an anxiety disorder may exist that requires professional attention. If your fear or anxiety is not at this level, then, like anger, reframing and other techniques can help you manage it. You can have power over this just as you can over anger.

Sadness and Despondency

A third troublesome emotional pattern or habit is that of pervasive sadness, melancholy, or despondency. We have all experienced these emotions at some point in our lives. But subclinical depression can be managed on your own if you have the motivation and use your personal resources. Again, cognitive reframing can help you overcome the effect of these feelings as can certain other things which apply components of EQ such as self-awareness and a belief in your ability to manage your own life. If you are despondent, you are likely to be pessimistic and negative in your thinking and difficult to live with. This can take a serious toll on an otherwise good marriage.

Even if you have severe depression and require psychotropic medication, you will nonetheless have to learn new skills, behavior patterns, attitudes, and emotional management that reflect EQ to keep yourself and your relationship healthy.

We are not passive victims to our feelings and emotions.

POSITIVE VS. NEGATIVE THINKING

Perhaps the most widely accepted link between managing your feelings/emotions and your thoughts is being positive, optimistic, and hopeful. Part of being emotionally intelligent is to maintain a hopeful attitude and thus generally suffer less than if you are pessimistic and feel hopeless. The same is true for having a sense of self-efficacy, which means you believe you are in charge of most of the outcomes of your life and have a sense of personal power to reach your goals and overcome obstacles.

If you are an efficacious person, you make a better marital partner. Self-efficacy is increased in part through success and personal mastery. Therefore, in your struggle to work out differences, the more you and your partner succeed in your individual lives in becoming who you aspire to be and succeed in improving your relationship together, the more personally powerful you will feel together—as a partnership.

Positive thinking has a major effect on your emotional and physical health and the overall outcome of your life. Most of us are capable of regulating our moods and can prolong pleasant moods and take charge of our minds by focusing on the positive things in life. You may be surprised at the effect this way of living has on your relationship/marriage.

Perhaps you have heard of the idea of having an "attitude of gratitude." The results of this are remarkable. You and your partner can benefit considerably from focusing on the "blessings" and positive things in your life together.

The following example demonstrates the effects of having an "attitude oɪ gratitude":

> Matt participated in group therapy for nearly a year to address residual anger toward an alcoholic father, a recent divorce, his own ongoing struggle with sobriety, difficulties with post-divorce dating relationships, depression for which he was taking a psychotropic drug, and an ongoing battle with self-esteem and career success. This very competent but angry and underachieving man was highly motivated to overcome these obstacles. Matt rather quickly became aware of his habit of negative thinking and patterns of "ain't it awful," "life is hopeless," and "I'm a failure." When I introduced the notion that he had some choice in whether he viewed life and his circumstances negatively or with more optimism and that he might consider maintaining an "attitude of gratitude," he felt like a lifeboat had been thrown to him. He proceeded to vigorously apply this to various aspects of his life and influenced other group members to adopt similar mindsets. It is no doubt naive to believe that adopting a positive attitude provides a magical cure for life's woes, but for Matt it clearly improved the quality of his life and opened doors for greater fulfillment. With inevitable brief setbacks, Matt was able to maintain more hope for his life, positive thinking, and a generally optimistic attitude. He maintained his sobriety with greater ease, was able to work through the anger toward his father, recovered more quickly than he anticipated from the ending of a love relationship, and made appropriate career changes.

Negative thoughts, interpretations, attitudes, and beliefs, if too pervasive, are toxic to your relationship. If you are a more negative person, you may expect the worst of your partner, interpreting his/her behavior as coming from a "bad motive." If you have a high level of hope and are more optimistic than pessimistic, you are more likely to interpret your partner's motives as coming from a constructive place. You are also more likely to be self-motivated, self-reassuring, and flexible and find ways to reach your goals.

With a positive attitude toward life, you can create interpersonal experiences that lead to better outcomes and greater rewards for yourself and your partner. When you relate positively to each other, you experience less stress and greater satisfaction together.

SUMMARY

Of the nine characteristics of EQ listed in Chapter 1, the five that are most essential for helping you know yourself and your partner better are:

1.   Being self-aware and having self-knowledge

2.   Maintaining hope, positive thinking, and an attitude of optimism

3.   Empathizing and being attuned to others, especially your partner, and dealing with them effectively

4.   Maintaining a sense of self-efficacy

5.   Knowing, understanding, and regulating or managing your emotions and expressing or using them appropriately and adaptively

These abilities and qualities are *italic* as they appear in the paragraphs that follow. Keep in mind that some of them overlap and build upon others.

To recognize and examine your basic personality qualities, your early life experiences, and the effects they have on who you have become and how you function in your adult life, be willing to fully know and understand yourself. This requires you to be open-minded and nondefensive regarding the truth of what you have experienced and what you truly feel, avoid denying what has occurred in your life, examine your memories, pay attention to how you present yourself, and listen attentively to the feedback of others who know and care about you. To deny any of this, refuse to acknowledge certain aspects of your personality, or brush aside influences with "my parents did the best they could" or "I am who I am and it doesn't matter how I got this way" interferes with genuine self-awareness.

Self-disclosure is also important in your relationship, but it is difficult without *self-awareness*. How can you disclose to your partner important things about yourself and what made you who you are if you don't really "know yourself"? This disclosure sometimes comes with strong emotions; therefore, the *use and appropriate expression of your emotions* or mood states are essential for self-disclosure to be safe. If you don't know what you are feeling, how you come across in expressing your feelings, or are oblivious to how you are acting, then misunderstandings and communication breakdowns are inevitable.

Your emotional states and the way you express them play a huge role in your relationship. It is your task as an emotionally intelligent adult to identify these and use them constructively. This effective use of emotions is a key factor in the process of sharing with and receiving information from your partner. You are unlikely to share personal or sensitive information with a partner who does not respond caringly.

Knowing how you feel at any given time, what motivates your particular feeling states, and how to effectively express them are all of utmost importance in self-development as well as in your interpersonal interactions.

The ability to be *hopeful, optimistic, and positive* undergirds nearly every relationship issue addressed in this book. As it applies to "Who Am I?: Beginning the Journey," it helps you accept your personality, your uniqueness, and the current and past experiences in your life. Negative, hopeless thinking keeps you mired down in a "victim mentality." This ability also provides you with a useful lens for viewing your partner.

Maintaining a sense of *self-efficacy* plays a role as well in overcoming a victim stance or a belief that "I am who I am and cannot change." You might think of this as having "a sense of personal power." If you are an efficacious person, you believe in your ability to influence outcomes in your life, achieve your goals, and overcome the inevitable obstacles you encounter along life's way.

If you have this quality, you will understand that you are who you are for a myriad of reasons and influences and that you have some degree of control over any change or growth from this point forward. This contributes immeasurably to the strength of your relationship because it gives you independence, confidence, and courage.

As an emotionally intelligent person, you remain hopeful about yourself but you also maintain a positive and hopeful attitude toward your partner. This leads to increased support, patience, and understanding in how you view and experience your partner's idiosyncrasies and struggles. Everyone has his/her own idiosyncrasies, and everyone brings "baggage" into a relationship. Hope and optimism are the "bellhops" that carry this often heavy baggage for us.

All of this has to be followed by an ability *to tune in to* your partner and express any *empathy* he/she may need. True *empathic and compassionate* interactions strengthen your bond. To patronize your partner with "this is just who you are," "well, you turned out OK," or "you can get over it" is *not* helpful or emotionally intelligent.

While *empathy and attunement* are related, they are different in some ways. In the context of this chapter, empathy may be necessary if, for example, your partner is dealing with something troublesome that affects his/her current life. Attunement is likely to help you more fully understand and accept why he/she has certain behaviors, feelings, or quirks. For example, the statement "You are just like your mother" can be delivered, heard, and interpreted in a myriad of ways.

Both *empathy and attunement* require you to have a genuine interest in your partner's feelings, beliefs, behaviors, experiences, and dreams. You cannot maintain a good connection if there is no interest in who this person truly is, what they have gone through, how they have come to be who they are, and how they are attempting to develop from here. One of the most powerful connectors in a relationship/marriage is to show genuine interest in your partner by getting outside of yourself and more tuned in to them.

Now that you understand the importance of getting to know yourself and your partner better, let's move on to something a bit more fun: friendship, companionship, intimacy, love, and sex. Chapter 3 will take you through these five key stages of your relationship and show you how EQ is essential to each one.

CHAPTER THREE

The "Fun"damentals
From Friendship to Sex

Humankind has done a marvelous job
of exploring outer space but a dismal
job of exploring our inner space.

—UN Secretary General Dag Hammarskjöld

A re you and your partner friends? Companions? Do you think you have an intimate relationship? How would you define "love"? And what about sex? Could you use some help there? Let's look at these levels of relating and see why emotional intelligence (EQ) is so necessary for maneuvering them.

FRIENDSHIP AND COMPANIONSHIP

Friendship

In many cases, friendship is the foundation of a long-lasting love relationship. This involves, among other things, the eleven items listed below. Use this as a checklist to determine whether you and your partner have a friendship.

- Confiding and self-disclosing with a sense of trust and without fear of reprisal or betrayal

- A willingness to be vulnerable

- Sharing of affection

- Spending time together and being companions

- Being honest but careful with criticism

- Showing emotional support

- Being loyal and defending your partner in his/her absence

- Being tolerant and accepting of each other's friends

- Communicating appreciation, expressing kindness, and being courteous to each other

- Engaging in regular conversation

- Accepting each other's uniqueness

Some of these are also aspects of intimacy, which is addressed later in this chapter. While women have typically viewed friendship as described above and men are more inclined to focus mostly on companionship, these stereotypes are changing. Men are increasingly expecting more of their relationships, including friendships. This is due to increased self-awareness and being more able to tune in to or be empathic with others.

Friendship is a good model for all intimate relationships. If you maintain close friendships and love your friends, you may be more able to sustain a long and fulfilling relationship/marriage. Frank Pittman, M.D., in his forthright book *Grow Up* says, "Get good at friendship before you even think about falling in love. Friendship is an infinitely more stabilizing basis for marriage than romance."[7]

Most long-term relationships/marriages eventually evolve to a point when friendship and/or companionship is the glue that holds them together. Many of us maintain or reignite passion as well, but we enjoy the stability of having our spouse as our "best friend" in our late middle and senior years.

This example demonstrates the value of friendship in a marriage:

Steve and Kathy had been married for 23 years. They had been able to share and communicate with each other on a consistent basis and enjoy some of the same interests. Both expressed a great appreciation for their ability to talk to each other and for the strength of their friendship. However, Kathy reached a point of dissatisfaction because she is a much more outgoing social person with a wider variety of interests than Steve, and she began to find him boring. Also they were unable to revive or maintain a romantic, passionate love relationship. And Kathy no longer found him sexually attractive. The strength of their friendship was not enough for her, and she made that ill-fated choice of dealing with this frustration by entering first one and later a second sexual affair outside their marriage. The couple considered divorce, and each chose to participate in a divorce recovery workshop separately. Over a period of time, I worked with them together as a couple and with each on an individual basis. Both achieved increased self-understanding and self-awareness and addressed deeper unresolved issues from their individual histories. Steve, who had been overly dependent on Kathy for friendship and companionship, learned to individuate. Kathy developed an appreciation for Steve. While friendship alone was not adequate for sustaining their marriage, it was ultimately the ingredient that provided the motivation to work out their other issues.

A long-term love relationship should include intimate conversation, personal and emotional connecting, and discussing "things that matter." This doesn't have to be done to excess, which can lead to an "intimacy overload" pattern. Your casual chitchat and day-to-day conversations are also a way of connecting and strengthening your bond.

Gottman reported in his best seller, *The Seven Principles for Making Marriage Work*, that when you connect with each other by engaging in regular chitchat, you are likely to stay happily married.

Real-life romance is fueled more by this humdrum approach to staying connected than the wild and passionate romance we see in the movies. If you can converse regularly about a wide variety of issues on a regular basis in a non-conflictual way, your relationship is strengthened.

You cannot have intimacy without conversation. To know and to love a friend, you must have regular talks. If a close relationship breaks down, it is likely to be because you quit talking, and a good friendship requires lots of time for talk. Talking with a friend requires self-awareness and being tuned in to the other person. It may also require managing your emotions, even if your conversations are not particularly "heavy."

Companionship

Companionship can be satisfying even if it is superficial because it involves spending time together and engaging in shared activities. You can do this without having deep verbal or emotional interactions. If you are content to participate in activities together and have no other expectations of your relationship, perhaps your level of EQ is less crucial. However, if your companionship involves activities requiring skill or strength and patience or tolerance or if there is a danger of competition, then such characteristics as empathy, attunement, self-motivation, and persistence in the face of frustration may be necessary.

The majority of people whose relationships are strained nonetheless continue to spend time doing things together. Whether or not you have children, spending quality time together is vital. If you are "outdoorsy," you could choose activities such as walking, bik-

Spending time doing things together which you both enjoy or are willing to share can have a healing quality.

ing, skiing, trips to the mountains, boating, camping, and fishing. And for those "indoor types," depending on your location, there might be an endless array of cultural events, athletic games, performing arts, dining out, and other opportunities for companionable time together. Ideally, you can learn to agree on mutually enjoyable activities or practice the art of taking turns and compromising in your companionship.

Sadly, sometimes your companionship can be laced with resentment and competition or silence and distance. If you are fortunate, you will rebuild connectedness by having fun together. Even in seemingly nonintimate activities you may be required to delay gratification, empathize, manage your feelings, read your mate's feelings, and regulate your moods. (EQ!)

I have developed a habit of observing couples having dinner together in restaurants. They appear to fall into five categories. Which one describes your relationship?

1. The deeply engaged, intimate couple

2. The friendly but superficial chitchat couple

3. The silent but peacefully together couple

4. The cold and distant couple

5. The openly hostile couple

The quality of your companionship can be reflected in these observable patterns.

INTIMACY

Do you think of sex when the notion of intimacy is introduced in conversation? While sex can be very intimate, it is not, in itself, intimacy. The key to real intimacy includes such things as those listed below.

Use this checklist to help you determine if your relationship is an intimate one.

- Regular personal conversation
- Familiarity with each other
- Commitment to confidentiality

A healthy dose of intimate connecting can lead to a satisfying sexual relationship.

- ○ **Emotional exposure**
- ○ **Mutual trust**
- ○ **Deep emotional sharing or connecting**
- ○ **Mutuality (not a one-sided connection)**
- ○ **Vulnerability**

Most authors do *not* include sexual relating in a definition or discussion of intimacy. Nearly all of us engage in sexual encounters as couples, but many of us do not have intimacy in our relationships. Some of us hardly know our partners and live with considerable distance between us. This is when the EQ qualities of attunement, self-understanding, and appropriate use of emotion can be helpful to you.

You can be happy and fulfilled even if you do not have a truly intimate relationship. Strange as it may seem, there are some couples who have an unstated agreement that intimacy is not a necessary ingredient for fulfillment. They appear to be content to relate at a more superficial level. However, for the majority of us, if our relationship is nonintimate, one or both of us eventually realizes that "something is missing" and gets to a point at which we need a greater depth of connecting.

Alex and Yolanda demonstrate this:

Alex and Yolanda had been in a committed relationship for four years when they came in for one session of couple therapy. Their relationship had been peaceful and companionable with few open conflicts, but it became apparent that it lacked emotional depth and intimacy. Neither was honest and clear with their needs, feelings, and expectations. Both were introverts, and there was minimal self-disclosure between them. Yolanda decided to leave the relationship. Each took my "When Your Relationship Ends" recovery workshop, and they continued to see each other weekly on a friendship basis. Alex, refusing to give up hope of a reconciliation, began to address his avoidance of intimate connecting and discomfort in dealing with deep personal issues. He reported that he shared his newfound self-awareness with Yolanda, and they began to practice more candid, honest interactions. Ultimately this couple ended their relationship, both claiming they learned a valuable lesson about sharing and connecting at a more intimate level in a committed relationship.

Generally speaking, women find it easier and more comfortable to maintain intimacy with others. Interestingly, men with high needs for intimacy are happier and better adjusted in work and marriage than men with low needs for intimacy. The need for intimacy has an energizing and growth-producing quality.

Each of the components of EQ can be applied to all of the issues addressed in this chapter. Let's focus our attention on three that are absolutely necessary for intimacy—the appropriate use and expression of feelings, self-awareness, and empathy/compassion. Each is explored here separately.

The Use of Feelings

Socrates' well-known injunction "know thyself" and the awareness of your own feelings as they occur are keystones to EQ. The expression of feelings is the key to intimate connecting. It is also important to note that the awareness of your feelings and acting to change them go hand in hand. You might find that identifying your feelings and then deciding to change some of them leads to a change in your behavior as well. This improves your interactions as a couple.

It is popular to claim that feelings are not to be judged and should be accepted just as they are. To a point this is true. You should not deny, discount, or suppress them. On the other hand, it is best not to be enslaved by your feelings and to mismanage or use them inappropriately. They enrich your experiences and bring color to your life, intellect, and personal interactions.

We are most human when we are aware of and able to operate out of our feelings.

Sometimes it is hard to identify or articulate what you are feeling and to manage this in a way that is appropriate in a given situation. Feelings that are too repressed can create distance and those extremely expressed can create havoc for you and your partner, preventing you from connecting at a deeper level.

The average person, when asked to define love, begins by saying, "It is a feeling that . . . " Clearly, mature love involves feelings, but it is not strictly a matter of having a feeling—it also involves understanding and managing your feelings, as well as reading and dealing effectively with others' feelings.

In general, if you know and manage your feelings well and read and deal effectively with other people's feelings, you perform better in all areas of your life.

In the past it was commonly held that your reasoning should not be influenced by emotions. The new paradigm blends your head and heart, so to speak. Feelings do add depth, spice, and richness to your life—to your experiences and relationships—different than what your intellect alone provides.

Despite the enlightenment of this modern era, there is an extraordinary lack of sharing of feelings in many current marriages.

You may be aware that you have feelings but may have trouble recognizing, naming, and expressing them appropriately. Needless to say, identifying your feelings is of limited value to your relationship/marriage if they are not shared with your partner.

And then there is the issue of over-emotionality. Some of us do not take things in stride and appear to thrive in a world of "trauma drama," or we react with strong emotion to most of the situations we encounter in life. While this may be expected of someone with a mental or psychological disorder, it is all too common and habitual in the general population. Although there are no hard and fast gender distinctions, men are more likely to have a tendency to react with anger or defensiveness when neither is called for and women with anxiety, fear, hurt, or exaggeration. Once you can identify this reaction as a "bad habit," in most cases it can be changed.

Self-Awareness

Self-awareness is also an essential ingredient of intimacy. You need to know not only your feelings but also your behaviors, thoughts, needs, beliefs, and motivations. If you really know and understand yourself, you are more adept at knowing and understanding your mate. Self-awareness is also the cornerstone to EQ. According to Goleman, it requires "attention to one's internal states . . . self-reflection, introspective attention to one's experience, including feelings . . . mindfulness. The fundamental skill of emotional intelligence is self-awareness . . . and self-awareness is fundamental to psychological insight."[8]

Understanding yourself is the first step to change. But many of us are at a loss when asked about our "inner selves" or "inner experiences." We have a hard time identifying our needs or motivations and accurately describing our actions, behaviors, or personalities.

Here is an example of the impact of this issue:

Alicia and Kevin entered couple therapy due to marital distress, which they attributed largely to differences in parenting styles. (This is often a "pre-senting" issue in marital discord but not the "real" issue.) Alicia grew up in a large family and was seven years old when her alcoholic father died. I found that Alicia was significantly lacking in self-awareness and could iden-tify no effect on her of her father's death and the resultant family strug-gles. As I worked with her, it became evident that she had mastered the use of denial in relation to her past as well as in her current marital situa-tion. She had always maintained an overinvolved relationship with their daughter, Elizabeth, an only child, and was very angry with Kevin for not being as attentive a father as she wanted him to be. She was unable to see a connection between this anger and the loss of her own father. Elizabeth, now 24 and still living at home, was demanding and disrespectful to which Alicia was blind for a time. Alicia had spent years doting on her husband and daughter to the denial of her own needs, and although she experi-enced great fear of living on her own, she eventually moved out. This was a tragic case of a woman simply unable to look deeper into her own feel-ings, experiences, motivations, and behaviors. Over time Alicia became more self-aware, and the couple continued to work to reconcile their mar-riage after a lengthy separation.

To understand yourself and be in touch with your "inner process" can re-quire daily, sometimes hourly, attention. It is not a goal to be achieved but a state to be experienced. Then you need to communicate this inner experience verbally to your partner to maintain closeness. True intimacy involves an ex-change—a mutual sharing—so listening to your partner is the other half of the equation.

One thing that interferes with your ability to empathize is self-absorption. If you are too self-focused (not the same as self-aware), you cannot get outside yourself enough to be empathic and compassionate. Self-absorption is com-

The ability to listen is the most important element of communication. And it is sorely lacking! Most couples seeking marital therapy feel their partner does not listen to them.

mon in one or both persons in many relationships, but there are degrees of severity. In its worst form, it can be narcissistic. This means a tendency to be arrogant, to overvalue your personal worth, to believe that you are "special and superior," and to have an excessive interest in your own comfort, appearance, abilities, and importance. While the full-blown narcissistic personality is relatively rare, self-absorption is quite common.

Don't confuse self-awareness and self-care with self-absorption. A self-absorbed person is less capable of true intimacy because it requires mutual sharing. Many of us do not achieve the closeness we desire because we are not mutually sharing or are defended against sharing. If one of us lacks self-understanding and tends to be self-absorbed, closeness is not possible.

A brief example demonstrates this:

Dolores and Mel experience a strong bond and were determined and motivated to save their marriage. This young couple came in for couple therapy with multiple issues—excessive conflict, difficulty in parenting their three children, and Dolores's distress over Mel's self-absorption. It is the latter that I address here. For reasons rooted in his personal psychological make-up, Mel was unable to identify or truly care about the needs of his three children and to some degree those of his wife. He was severely lacking in the EQ quality of attunement and was only willing to be truly invested in things that were of interest to him. It was a burdensome chore to take the children to their various activities, participate in household responsibilities, and even focus on what his wife was saying when she spoke to him. Although not classically narcissistic, he simply could not listen to her because he was overly caught up in himself. Admittedly, Dolores was a strong-minded, very expressive person who "got on his case" quite often. But this was more than a simple power struggle. Through two series of treatments, this couple was finally able to reduce their conflict, improve communication, and establish a more mutually satisfying relationship. Mel was able to recognize his self-absorption and improve his ability to tune in to Dolores, while she learned that being angry with him did not achieve her sought-after goal of increased partnering.

Empathy and Compassion

The third quality of emotional intelligence that is necessary for intimacy is the ability to empathize and show compassion for your partner. Do you and your partner tune in to and show genuine caring for each other?

Do not confuse empathy with sympathy. To be empathic with your part-ner is to be able to "wear their moccasins" or "enter their world." It is feeling with and for your partner without getting pulled into pitying or codepen-dence. You will usually experience less anxiety, frustration, hurt, and the like when you feel truly heard, understood, and cared for. While you cannot be your spouse's therapist, you can certainly be present in a way that is caring. What better way to be intimate?

"Empathy builds on self-awareness; the more open we are to our own emo-tions, the more skilled we will be in reading feelings. All rapport, the root of caring, stems from emotional attunement, from the capacity for empathy. (Those who have) . . . empathy skills . . . have better relationships with the op-posite sex. Empathy, it should be no surprise to learn, helps with romantic life."[9] More of Goleman's wisdom.

Do you feel like you partner really hears you, understands you, and is there for you? If so, you are very fortunate. If either of you lack the ability to be em-pathic and compassionate, you will not be attuned to your partner. Fortunately the ability to be empathic can be acquired. In many of us, it is developed in infancy; if not, it can be learned. It is nearly impossible to "fake" empathy. Being truly empathic requires you to be genuine, to listen carefully, to have a nonjudgmental attitude, and to accept whatever your partner is experiencing or saying.

Here is an example of this effort:

Donna is an individual who has wisely chosen to continue her individual therapy off and on for many years—initially for the purpose of healing and then for continued personal growth. And her EQ has increased to an ad-mirable level! I worked with her through the healing of early life wounds, career struggles, the ending of her marriage, ongoing spiritual development issues, and maintaining healthy love relationships. She became involved ap-proximately three years ago with a man who had all the qualities she felt she needed in a partner emotionally, spiritually, and physically. They com-municate well, handle disagreements effectively, and are good compan-ions. But there is one potential flaw. Michael has a strong genetic proclivity to alcoholism, and his early life experiences have made him a good candi-date for this disease. He does not have a serious, consistent drinking pat-tern, but Donna becomes very anxious when he drinks. She readily admits a tendency toward perfectionism and a need for the "ideal life and the ideal partner" but has recently decided to approach Michael's "problem" with compassion and empathy. She is attempting to understand that alcoholism is a disease that he did not choose and that he is making every effort to maintain sobriety and not let his struggle contaminate their relationship. She is becoming aware that alcoholics have a right to committed love relationships but is learning how to establish boundaries to ensure that her needs are met. While trying to be compassionate and empathetic, Donna is careful to avoid a mindset of denial, which is all too common among partners and family members of alcoholics. Time will tell.

Volumes could be written on these and other ingredients of intimacy. Suffice it to say that if you are self-aware, empathic or compassionate, and use your feelings appropriately, this can radically deepen and enrich your intimate connections.

LOVE

We can be quite naive about love and its meaning or role in our adult relationships. Have you or someone you know said that you married because you were "in love," or insisted that you need to leave a relationship because you are no longer "in love"? Surely you have heard the expression, "I love you, but I'm not *in* love with you."

> *The concept of love is perhaps the most misunderstood and complex of all the components of committed relationships.*

The media, in all its forms, and culture in general promote a romanticized and inaccurate notion of what love is in a committed relationship.

This section is unique in that it includes excerpts from several experts that contribute to our understanding of love. You will find it interesting and instructive that each suggests a more mature and emotionally intelligent approach to love. Read each of these carefully and locate your own views and any misconceptions you may have about love.

Erich Fromm, Ph.D.[10]

* Love is not just a pleasant sensation, a matter of chance, something you "fall into."

- We are preoccupied with being in love and not concerned enough with being loving.

- Love is not easy.

Harville Hendrix, Ph.D.[11]

- Love is a creation of our unconscious mind based on unfinished business with our parents.

- Romantic love thrives on ignorance, fantasy, projection, denial, and an ideal image of who our partner is.

- We need to love in a more mature way by being more conscious.

Frank Pittman, M.D.[12]

- The manic high of the "in love" state has little to do with loving, and the absence of it is not grounds for divorce.

- "Romantic love" may be delicious, but it is an absurd escape from sanity—a narcissistic intoxication with no relationship to loving.

- If you want to recapture that magic from when you were "in love," be loving.

M. Scott Peck, M.D.[13]

- Love is too large and deep to be understood or measured by words.

- We fall in love only when we are consciously or unconsciously sexually motivated.

- Falling in love is temporary.

- Sooner or later we fall out of love if the relationship lasts long enough.

Leo Buscaglia, Ph.D.[14]

- If you attempt to define love, you run the danger of being vague or nebulous and arriving nowhere.

- We do not fall into or out of love, but instead we grow in love.

- Real love requires flexibility, sensitivity, understanding, tolerance, knowledge, and strength.

John Gottman, Ph.D.[15]

- A healthy, successful, lasting marriage is not created by a romanticized view of love based on passion and a powerful "in love" feeling.

- Love is tied to respect and includes affection, pride in one's partner, showing genuine interest in each other's lives, and having empathy.

- Mature love requires that you seek out and respect each other's opinions and views, listen carefully, and care about each other's feelings.

Marianne Williamson[16]

- Love is not something that takes our pain away but brings it to the surface and demands skills in compassion, acceptance, and forgiveness.

- "Falling in love" offers a brief period of seeing the perfection in a loved one, but craziness sets in quickly.

Susan Johnson, Ed.D.[17]

- Adult love is an emotional tie that provides a secure base, safe haven, and source of comfort and caring.

- The bond or attachment in a marriage has to be carefully managed for it to be a mature exchange of love.

- It is the appropriate management of feelings that is the key to this bond or attachment.

And so it goes—expert after expert reinforcing the notion that we must be more mature in our view of what love is. We have to deepen our self-knowledge, be truly attuned to our partner, manage our emotions more maturely, maintain a sense of optimism when things change, and persist when those "in love" feelings fade.

Romantic love may be an important first step in drawing us together. However, it is not that upon which you base your foundation. In a recent lecture Jeffrey Zeig, Ph.D., founder/director of the Milton Erickson Foundation, described love with the acronym TOPIAH:

Taking

Obvious

Pleasure

In

Another's

Happiness

SEX

When you bring up the issue of sex, you are likely to refer to it as intimacy. This appears to be true for both men and women. Sex can sometimes be intimate and intimacy can include sex, but the terms cannot be interchanged because they are distinct in meaning.

A sexual relationship between consenting adults should involve synchronicity, rapport, and mutual empathy. If you have the EQ to achieve these things, you are more likely to be fulfilled and happy in your sex life.

Many of us are "touch starved." What happens between you and your partner with nonsexual affection? If your partner reaches for your hand more often than he reaches for your breast or gives you a sweet kiss on the cheek more often than a forceful tongue, you are much more likely to welcome his approach and be comfortable with his touch. This can be an issue for both men and women. We are sometimes too focused on sex and not enough on affection. An increase in nonsexual affection usually increases your comfort with physical contact and ultimately your sexual interactions.

Sex is vital to most couples, but it is by no means always a show of affection. As a matter of fact, there appears to be a trend toward improving "technique" and just having sex instead of making love. Stressing mechanics and performance can be destructive to your committed love relationship. It may be appropriate for "casual" relationships but not for your marriage. Focusing on satisfying your raw sexual needs and not on tenderness, sharing, or pleasing does little to deepen things between the two of you.

It is rare for a serious relationship to be destroyed by sexual incompatibility, despite some couples' claims. If your sexual problems appear to be destructive, this is more likely to be caused by not understanding your role in the process, not delaying your own gratification, poor management of your emotions, not being tuned in to your own or your partner's needs and feelings, or not expressing those needs and feelings. In other words, certain qualities of EQ are essential for negotiating the complexities of physical closeness and sex.

The role and dynamics of sex can be as complex and misunderstood as the concept of love. Despite the easy availability of sexual material in this culture and the mass media, many of us lack fundamental knowledge about sex and do not fully understand our own needs or the anatomy and sexual response of our partner. And yet even the issues of knowledge and technique do not get to the heart of what is most important in sexual relating.

The intimacy needs of many (though not all) men are met through sexual interaction. It is also common for men to equate sexual encounters with being or feeling loved. Gender studies make it clear that it is the socialization process that has created this.

Sexuality is, after all, a form of energy, a natural drive. But what we overlook is that it can be redirected or rechanneled into other expressions. Focusing too much on sex and not being resourceful in finding joy or pleasure in other constructive and satisfying outlets can create a serious problem in your sexual relationship.

The more sophisticated or evolved and emotionally intelligent person is less likely to succumb to this overfocus on sex. For example, if you really know yourself, are genuinely interested in your partner's needs, can delay your own gratification, can control your impulses, and can communicate effectively, you will function more maturely when it comes to sex. Broadening your source of pleasure can reap rich rewards.

Women may be more likely to give in to a lack of initial desire and unwillingness to have sex with their partners on a consistent basis. In part, this problem is purely physical or biological. Women in many cases are not as easily stimulated sexually as are men and may have to "work harder." Just as a man can learn to redirect excessive sexual desire and broaden his sources of pleasure in life, a woman can choose to increase her desire and the frequency of sexual contact. A woman can learn to relax and give her partner a chance to participate in her arousal, even though initially she may have little or no interest.

As is true for men, a more emotionally intelligent woman will make this effort to contribute to a mutually satisfying sex life. Being empathetic to your partner's need or desire for sex, expressing your own feelings about this in an appropriate and nonrejecting way, and getting to know your own sexual needs can go a long way toward mutual satisfaction.

Your sexual energy and the urge to have sex are as natural as the desire to survive and the need to eat. You may experience times when you are out of touch with this energy and will have to work to activate it. This may be more common among women, but a surprising number of men also need to "activate" their libidos.

Sex can help you appreciate and accept each other. It can be one method of deeply connecting that is not present in your other close or important relationships. It is a sensitive issue and can be disastrous if it is not handled appropriately.

You and your partner should discuss sex and your sexual needs directly and openly. Ask gently for what you want, create a mutually safe environment, and don't respond to requests for change in a defensive manner. Requests are not criticism. You can have a happy intimate sex life, but be careful not to take the expression of different needs or desires as personal insults. This acceptance requires maturity and EQ.

I like the no-nonsense and forthright approach of Frank Pittman. In *Grow Up*, he says, "Sex is good for you and good for your marriage . . . Couples should do it regularly whether they want to or not. Foreplay should start the day before . . . and work for both people (so that) each gets what he or she wants from it . . . Couples can remain sexually active for a lifetime if they don't turn it into a competitive sport. Over a lifetime, sex requires wondrous amounts of both humility and goodwill and a fair amount of communication. Honestly, if you don't use it, you really will lose it."[18] While Pittman does not directly address the issue of EQ, it is implicit in his call for humility, goodwill, maturity, and the mutual meeting of needs.

Broaden your view of sex to include the entire realm of sensuality and mutual pleasure derived through your senses. Your body can be used for warmth and closeness, which requires candid communication. The ability to maintain this broad view of sex also requires maturity, delayed gratification, the ability to control impulses, emotion management, and being able to handle frustration.

Mature sex involves more than the purely physical. It can be a real challenge to sustain sexual enjoyment with the same partner over a period of years if you don't make new discoveries together and find ways to enrich your sex life. This involves finding new potential in yourself and your partner, and making it more satisfying for both of you.

I have found that women often feel better about themselves when they communicate their sexual needs to their partners. It is important to both give and receive pleasure, and this requires a strong sense of self by both the giver and the receiver. It also requires loving or accepting your body. If you see your body as ugly or unacceptable, it will be difficult to relax, enjoy the encounters, believe you deserve pleasure, and feel comfortable giving or receiving. This is generally more of a problem for women than it is for men because of the pressure from society to have the perfect body. If you hide in the dark or under the covers, your sexual connection is compromised.

One key to a good sex life is a belief that you deserve pleasure and have a willingness to receive it.

A self-esteem problem for men shows up as a tendency to be defensive and have a "bruised ego" when partners give feedback and ask for certain changes. How else are we to relate our sex needs to each other if we don't communicate honestly and openly? This can be a major stumbling block to a mature, satisfying encounter. A word of caution to both men and women—when stating your sexual needs, be sure to do it gently and sensitively (empathy and attunement).

SUMMARY

While all nine of the EQ characteristics considered could apply to the issues in this chapter, the following are perhaps the most essential.

- **Empathizing and being attuned to others, especially your partner, and dealing with them effectively**

- Knowing, understanding, and regulating or managing your emotions and expressing or using them appropriately and adaptively

- Delaying gratification and controlling or resisting your impulses, both emotionally and in actions

- Maintaining persistence in the face of frustration

- Being self-aware and having self-knowledge

- Maintaining a sense of self-efficacy

Superficial interactions do not usually require the appraisal or effective handling of emotions, but other aspects of EQ do play a role in many friendships. For example, companionship that is strictly activity-focused can be satisfying without the presence of *empathy or attunement*; however, if a friendship is deeper, these qualities are important. Clearly, any such close friendship requires the exchange of empathy and an adequate amount of mutual attunement or dealing with one another's emotions.

Likewise, intimacy, as described in this chapter, requires you to be empathic and tuned in to your partner. If you develop more intimacy with your partner, you will be generally more fulfilled. *Being attuned* to each other helps in many ways.

Love, that rascally and difficult to define experience, is not just a collection of feelings—it requires you to be able to deal with one another's emotions effectively. If you want your love to be mature, it needs to be infused with mutual *empathy and attunement*. We do not live in a fairy tale world, and our need for the expression of love cannot always be met upon demand. When we are going through a period in which we do not "feel" much love for our partner, an emotionally intelligent partner can stand back and not be devastated by these feelings.

Genuine intimacy and mature adult love also require both of you to have the ability to identify what you are feeling, to keep your feelings from spinning out of control, and to convey them effectively to each other. While there are millions of marriages that exist without genuine intimacy, these couples are likely to be struggling in either an arid desert of emotion or in unnecessary pain and chaos.

Sexual relating, one of the more complex issues between couples, flows more smoothly if your interactions are accompanied by empathy and attunement. Sex and intimacy are different experiences, but it is being really tuned in that brings your sexual interactions to a deeper and more satisfying level. To have a healthy sex life, try to understand and empathize with each other's feelings and needs.

Unquestionably, the ability to *delay gratification, control your impulses,* and *persist when you are frustrated* are aspects of EQ that apply to sex. Sometimes your partner is not as interested in sex as you are, and you may feel sexually deprived and frustrated. While the "deprived" partner is usually the male, this is not always the case. Essentially the *delay of gratification and persistence* is necessary while you are negotiating a workable sexual interaction that satisfies the needs of both.

All four major levels of relationships discussed in this chapter—friendship, intimacy, love, and sex—require *self-awareness* and *self-knowledge.* Throughout this text these qualities of EQ are presented as key components or cornerstones of your interactions. If you want friendship, intimacy, love, and sex with your partner, continue to work at getting to know and understand yourself.

This also helps with *self-efficacy* because the more you really know yourself, the more likely you are to believe you have some power and control over the outcomes of your life. When you are maneuvering through these levels of relating, you need to feel this sense of personal power.

•   •   •

Let's move on to how you can handle some of the most common stumbling blocks faced by couples. You will see how important your EQ is in expressing your needs, honoring those of your partner, handling your differences, and managing conflict. Chapter 4 gives you the hope that nearly any difficulty can be overcome or situation improved if you have the right attitude and apply the right tools.

CHAPTER FOUR

The Power of "We"

Nothing great was ever achieved
without enthusiasm.

—RALPH WALDO EMERSON

"The problem with our relationship is that we don't communicate very well." "I don't understand him/her. I can't figure out what he/she needs." "We fight too much. I get tired of all the fighting." "I can never win an argument with her/him."

As you know, many couples claim that they have "communication problems" and they "fight too much." While this may in fact be true, these are symptoms of something more complex, such as having difficulty in expressing your needs or honoring those of your partner, not having enough tolerance for your style and personality differences, or lacking true intimacy.

If you want to get your needs met, meet your partner's needs, respect the differences between you, and manage your conflict better, this chapter will help you. If you can be persistent, deal with frustration in a mature way, tolerate the inevitable defeats and setbacks, maintain empathy for your partner, stay positive and hopeful, and be aware of your own style and needs, anything is possible. This is what gives power to the "we" in partnering.

IDENTIFYING, EXPRESSING, AND HONORING NEEDS

You may have been raised in an environment in which expressing your needs was encouraged and allowed, or was it just the opposite? Some parents are very tuned in to and welcoming of children expressing their needs. Others are disinterested in what children really need and are oblivious or disapproving of such openness. Likewise, you may have seen your parents mutually share what they needed and respond caringly or just the opposite. If they were good role models with this process, count your blessings!

As you proceed, remember that emotions or feelings are intricately linked to how and what you need. Which of these apply to you?

○ I can identify what I need and state my needs easily.

○ I find that when I state my needs clearly, my partner responds well.

○ I have spent a lifetime so out of touch with my needs that I am unable to identify them.

○ I have difficulty identifying what I need because I just don't think about it.

○ I believe that stating my needs is selfish and demanding.

○ I don't have a right to have my needs met.

○ I fear that my needs are not likely to be understood and met anyway, so why bother?

○ I get into "needs contests" or tugs-of-war in which I refuse to honor those needs of my partner because he/she will not meet mine.

Honestly identifying your opinions, preferences, and motivations and "publishing" them kindly to your partner improves the flow of communication and understanding. Although there are few hard and fast gender distinctions, men are more likely to be unable or unwilling to identify needs and feelings because doing so is viewed as weakness or vulnerability; however, they will express opinions and preferences.

At the same time women are somewhat more likely to share feelings than to express needs and opinions. Both women and men have to watch out for overaccommodating and overcommitting to others, which can lead to martyrdom. Even if you are clear on what you need, feel, prefer, or believe, whether man or woman, you may lack the ability to express these feelings appropriately or with emotional intelligence (EQ).

Here is an illustration of this:

Sean entered therapy due to depression; but it quickly became evident that he was playing a subservient role to Karen, his wife of 10 years, for fear of losing her. He took the role of martyr in their marriage and denied his personal and relationship needs, as well as his right to express them. Sean was the oldest child in his family of origin and had been given the responsibility of caring for his siblings while little attention was paid to his own needs by himself or his parents. He married a woman whom he "put on a pedestal" and to whom he felt inferior, but his self-effacing style and lack of self-care interfered with her respect for him. Through several months of therapy with Sean and Karen, both individual and extensive couple therapy, he began to experience increased self-awareness and self-esteem. He developed interests of his own and began to see that it was important for him to identify and express his needs. Although it was terrifying for him to face the possibility of losing his wife, he began to take the risk of standing up for himself. Sean recently reported that they were doing well and that he had been able to maintain his self-awareness and self-confidence as well as a newly found comfort in expressing his needs.

Generally speaking, as a self-aware individual, you are more likely to be able to manage both your emotions and your behaviors and know what you are thinking, doing, sensing, or needing. It is better if you are able to name or describe these things than if they are vague, you are oblivious to them, or they go unstated.

Even decision making, whether it is about a major life issue such as a career change or a less dramatic issue such as how to respond to being hurt by your partner, is easier and more sound if you are honestly attuned to what it is you desire, your internal states, and how you are behaving.

If you can look at all of these aspects of yourself realistically, you are less likely to be self-absorbed or narcissistic. You will also be better able to "get inside" your partner's feelings or needs and display that important quality of attunement.

Calvin and Denise demonstrate this struggle:

Calvin cycled through a somewhat narcissistic self-absorption early in his marriage, thinking primarily of his own needs and interests but ultimately taking a role of submission to his wife, allowing her to berate him. He grew up with a very self-absorbed father who expected him to begin working at an early age and to take care of most of his own needs, both materially and emotionally. Determined to make it on his own, Calvin grew up to become a world-class athlete and was successful in his career. After ten years of marriage, his wife, Denise, grew tired of his self-absorption and began to assert herself (at times with inappropriate aggression), which ultimately resulted in a separation and near-divorce. Through several months of therapy, both individually and together, Denise and Calvin deepened their self-awareness and were both able to recognize that they were playing out some destructive patterns from their histories. Calvin went from being very self-centered to an extreme opposite of self-efface-ment and a sense of hopelessness about himself. He was ultimately able to strike a healthy balance and as Denise continued to address the root of her anger and hurt, they proceeded, although cautiously, toward healing the marriage.

One of the earliest skills you may have learned as an infant, according to developmental psychologists, was the ability to modulate your feelings and soothe yourself. According to Bowlby, world-renowned leader in the field of attachment, emotionally sound infants learn to soothe themselves by treating themselves as their caretakers have. Ideally, if you are soothed or nurtured properly as an infant, you learn to replicate this behavior and will be better pre-pared to soothe and nurture yourself and modulate your emotions in adult-hood. This is a valuable EQ quality to use in your relationship.

Many of us make wrong choices of adult love partners because we don't know what we need or what is appropri-ate for us, and we can suffer years in these relationships. Although you might be able to change and save your relationship/marriage with effective help and hard work, it may be that you and your partner should never have been together in the first place. It does re-quire really knowing your needs and being able to work effectively with your emotions to make an appropriate choice of a partner.

If you understand yourself, what follows is an increased ability to manage your behavior and treat yourself well.

Some of you may identify your needs easily and comfortably and state these to others, including your partner. But what if this does not come naturally or easily to you? This ability can be de-veloped. Examples of some of the things required for this process are listed below. Use this as a checklist to deter-mine your readiness in this area.

Once you get clear on what you need and can identify your feelings and opinions, the next step is to "publish" them to your partner.

- ○ **Assertiveness or ability to speak up**

- ○ **Willingness to take the risk that you may not get desired results**

- ° Self-confidence

- ° Conviction or belief that you have a right to state your needs, feelings, and opinions

- ° Appropriate, nondemanding communication

- ° Overcoming the fear of the closeness that may result

All of these characteristics are reflective of some aspect of your EQ!

You are more likely to be heard and your needs or feelings responded to if you publish or deliver them appropriately. To do this requires effective communicating. One of the most common mistakes we make is to use complaints instead of stating our requests. Stop and think about whether you try to get what you want in your relationship/marriage by complaining or criticizing your partner instead of just clearly stating what you need. This is extremely important!

Whether it is about yourself or about your partner, self-talk can be powerful in influencing your thoughts and feelings.

Appropriate self-talk is also important, but don't let your self-talk be negative, self-deprecating, or counterproductive.

What if you make the effort to identify your needs and take the risk to express them to your partner and he/she discounts or refuses to honor them? In general, if your needs are reasonable (admittedly this is subjective), it is your partner's responsibility to respond appropriately. Ideally he/she will be emotionally available to you and responsive to your requests. To function well in this area, you will both have to listen attentively, be empathic and capable of attunement, and be self-confident enough to give to each other.

Stop and make a list of the things you know you need in your marriage. I'm certain I need:

1. The assurance that my partner is trustworthy

2. Affection

Continue to list 10 or more.

RESPECT FOR AND TOLERANCE OF DIFFERENCES

Generally speaking, for a variety of reasons, you consciously or unconsciously choose a partner who is significantly different than you. However, once you commit to that other person and pass through the honeymoon or romance stage, you are forced to face the reality of these differences. Your differences may not cause great discomfort or conflict or they may be so insurmountable that they contribute to the demise of your relationship. Ironically, the very characteristics, habits, and traits that we find attractive in a potential partner and that drew us in are ultimately the things we claim "drive us mad" and which we find intolerable.

No two people are alike, and so it is inevitable and unavoidable to find at least some differences between yourself and your partner. Sometimes these are relatively minor differences involving such things as taste in food. Others are much more significant such as having hugely dissimilar value systems. You may be tolerant or intolerant of your partner's way of doing things and/or their beliefs, habits, and personality traits. With many couples, one or the other tries to "remake the partner in their own image" (although this is often vehemently denied). It is easy to get stuck in the mode of thinking there is only one appropriate way to be and to do things. This is when tolerance, positive and optimistic thinking, and managing your own emotions come in very handy. EQ!

Some of the most common issues with which you might struggle due to personality or style differences are listed below. Which of these apply to you?

- Approaches to parenting or relating to children

- The underresponsible/overresponsible dilemma

- The overly emotional/underemotional dichotomy

- The laid-back vs. uptight difference

- The introverted or quiet personality vs. the extroverted or outgoing and social one

- The organized and clean approach vs. the disorganized and messy

- Specific gender differences

There are many other issues on which you may disagree, but they may be more related to differences of opinion and not necessarily personality or style differences.

You can learn to deal with these differences peacefully. If you are highly motivated, you can make significant changes quickly. Paula and Allen's story demonstrates this process:

Paula and Allen came in presenting with every one of the issues listed above and a couple of other concerns as well. Allen was not very invested in their three small sons, yet they were the most important part of Paula's life. Paula was fussy and compulsive with the house and more high strung, while Allen neglected helping with domestic chores and had a very laid-back style. Paula liked going out and socializing; Allen hated to dress up and go out. She was Protestant; he Catholic. Allen drank more than was comfortable for Paula, and she drank very little. She was very affectionate, and he not affectionate at all. Far more damaging to their marriage than their many differences was the fact that they did not discuss things, did not sit and process their feelings, did not express their needs, and avoided all conflict. Remarkably, within six sessions this couple was experiencing a satisfaction in their marriage that they had never felt. They each became more self-aware and were able to discuss their differences and problems. Allen stopped drinking and began to enjoy spending more quality time with their children. They began going out together a bit more. Allen made a major improvement in helping around the house. They began going to church together and were planning to begin a fitness program together. Both showed a sincere desire to be more attuned to the other, to express their own needs and feelings, and to respond empathically to those of their partner. Allen became more affectionate and although they did not show an increased comfort with conflict and continued to avoid fighting with each other, this did not appear to interfere with their ability to talk things through and resolve differences. All too familiar? Sound too easy? In a follow-up call to this couple five months later, they were continuing to maintain these changes. This couple was not "incompatible." They simply needed to relate to each other in a more emotionally intelligent way.

Is it a foreign idea to you that differences should be valued and honored? Actually, differences between you and your partner do not cause so-called "incompatibility." It is your inability to discuss them effectively and to problem-solve that gets in the way. In reality, these differences can produce growth and provide richness and texture to your interactions. Much conflict and fighting in your relationship/marriage is the result of resisting or not accepting your partner as different than yourself.

Do you tend to criticize or discount your partner for acting, thinking, believing, or feeling in a way that is different than yours? If this criticism becomes harsh and consistent and if your differences are not respected, your rela-

It's not what you disagree about but how you disagree that creates difficulties.

tionship may be in danger. Research on the dangers of criticism proves how destructive it can be. Over time you may despise your partner, which can ultimately destroy your relationship.

A driving force behind intolerance of differences is fear. You may feel, " If _____ does not do _____ my way, then I fear _____ will happen. If we are too different in our styles and habits, then _____ might result." I invite you to fill in these blanks with several examples that may apply to you and your partner. To do this exercise, it is important to think about the fears that are behind your intolerance; however, this can take a lot of thought. It's not always easy to identify these feelings.

Pittman, in *Grow Up*, contributes these words of wisdom to this dilemma, "You don't have to be perfect, your partner doesn't have to be perfect, but you do have to be fully there."[19] And to be frightened or threatened by your partner being different than you is not being fully there!

Don't give up too easily. Sometimes we are either so frightened or so short-sighted that we will end a relationship when one or two qualities are missing in a partner or in the relationship even though there are many positives. If you persist when you are frustrated with your partner, show tolerance for his/her weaknesses, avoid letting your negative emotions guide your thinking, truly tune in, and express your feelings and needs appropriately, such use of EQ may possibly save your relationship.

A brief example illustrates this struggle:

Paul was highly educated; Deb was not. They had been good compan-ions, shared similar values, raised a family, and had similar living style preferences. It was Deb's lack of a formal education that Paul ultimately used as an excuse for developing a relationship with another woman. He claimed that Deb was not intellectually challenging enough and that this affected his physical attraction to her, and so the couple separated and ultimately divorced. As a result of this rejection, Deb returned to college and began to examine her other relationships. It turned out that most of her long-time friends were highly educated individuals who had always found her quite stimulating, and she ultimately developed a new love relationship with another highly educated man. I do not share this case to belittle the value of a need for intellectual stimulation in a marriage or to deny that it can affect respect for one's partner but to point out the shortsightedness that can lead to the demise of an otherwise good relationship. This is often accompanied by the rejecting partner being arrogant and implying that their mate is less than perfect and that they themselves are not.

Gender studies reveal that, generally speaking, men and women can be different when it comes to dealing with rocky emotions. It has been found that men tend to experience emotions less intensely than women. And women can communicate more comfortably on a personal level. If you are objective and work with these differences, the gap between you and your partner need not be an obstacle. Men and women have a great deal to learn from each other. Each of us can borrow from the other—we are moving closer to the middle, wherein lies respect and tolerance.

CONFLICT

Seldom, or perhaps never, does a marriage
develop into a relationship smoothly and
without crises; there is no coming into
consciousness without pain.

—CARL JUNG, M.D.

A key ingredient of success in your relationship/marriage is the ability to persist despite inevitable difficulties and the wisdom to acknowledge that relationships by their very nature can be fraught with conflicts and problems. Where communication skills and EQ are most needed is in the arena of conflict and handling differences. When you say, "we have communication problems," you are probably saying that "we don't know how to handle our differences or settle our conflicts."

There are a number of excellent resources for conflict management in relationships. *The Power of Two* by Susan Heitler, Ph.D., is a good example. It provides the fundamentals of dialogue in marriage, dealing with anger, conflict resolution, shared decision making, and other communication or conflict-related issues.

> *The myth of "if we loved each other, this wouldn't be difficult" is just that—a myth.*

What follows are brief statements on six issues that show you the importance of using EQ in the face of conflict. These include probing and questioning for information, managing anger in yourself and your partner, stopping the blame game, listening is loving, sharing the problem, and incompatibility.

Probing and Questioning for Information

Having the ability to probe and ask questions appropriately can go a long way in helping you to manage conflict with your mate. You can ward off unnecessary and destructive interactions by asking your partner appropriate questions—to seek more information about what they are saying, feeling, or doing. If he/she says something potentially inflammatory, you can ask defensively, "What do you mean by THAT?" or you can say in a peacemaking tone, "Can you tell me more about what you are feeling . . . or saying . . . or . . . needing?" or "Say more about that." or "I honestly don't understand. Can you please clarify?"

Some of the frustration you feel with each other is due to a lack of necessary information. If you slow down, probe, ask questions, and get clarity, you can prevent a lot of tension, hurt, and misunderstanding.

An emotionally intelligent person can pause, even in the heat of battle, to probe for further information and genuinely listen to responses. You can persist even if you are frustrated, control

> *It is when we are angry that the gathering of information is most needed.*

your impulses in both your actions and emotions, maintain an optimistic attitude, and be empathic toward your partner.

Are you thinking this is impossible to do when you are angry? Not so. It may take a healthy dose of self-awareness and management of emotion, but it's worth it. When you are angry, stop and ask a *good* question! Use your EQ!

Managing Anger in Yourself and Your Partner

Anyone can become angry—that is easy. But to be
angry with the right person, to the right degree, at
the right time, for the right purpose, and in the
right way—this is not easy.

—ARISTOTLE

Many emotional reactions that are triggered in your adult relationships were learned in your childhood or demonstrated by your parents. It goes without saying that you need to learn or relearn to manage your own strong emotions as adults. What is often overlooked but needs to be considered is how you handle the anger or other strong emotions of your partner.

Many of us unknowingly take on or overreact to the emotions of others and tend to recreate their moods in ourselves.

Goleman calls this "emotional contagion" and "mood synchronicity." Helping your partner to soothe his/her feelings is a valuable skill and can bring you closer. This kind of connection between the two of you is what leads to attunement, one of the nine key EQ qualities. If you are good at being in tune with each other's moods, your emotional interactions will go more smoothly. On the other hand, if you are ineffective in the way you send and receive emotional messages to each other, you are likely to feel at odds with each other.

Having this ability to calm and to manage distressing emotions in a mate " . . . allows one to shape an encounter . . . thrive in intimate relationships, and put (them) at ease" (Goleman).[20]

Clearly you need to learn how to react to strong emotions in your partner and follow his/her ups and downs, particularly in dealing with anger. However, if taken too far, this situation can lead to codependency and do more harm than good. A codependent person is one who allows the behaviors and emotions of others to have an overly powerful effect on them and who is caught up in believing they can somehow control or change others. They get lost in the feelings and actions of those around them and do not maintain adequate personal ego boundaries between themselves and others.

There is a "codependent dance" in most relationships. Look back at the definition of codependency and ask yourself how it applies to you as a couple.

In the process of connecting emotionally, you have to give up the illusion

> To calm, inspire, or put your partner at ease promotes connecting and desired closeness.

that you can somehow change or control your partner's behaviors, attitudes, or emotions. The goal is to be *inter*dependent not *co*dependent. The anger and other strong emotions that come with your conflicts and disagreements are handled more effectively if you are both able to be tuned in and empathetic without creating an unhealthy entanglement.

There are many books, workshops, and classes on anger management. Whether on your own or through using one of these resources, you can learn to self-regulate when it comes to your emotions. Ask yourself how well you currently apply the following self-regulating techniques:

- **Accept responsibility for and choose your own emotional responses**

- **Reframe situations from being stressful or anger producing to being challenging or growth enhancing**

- **Be aware of and manage your own emotional triggers**

If left unmanaged, your anger can develop into rage or result in verbal, emotional, or physical abuse. We all react with different emotions to different situations and this is when self-awareness is essential.

The following situation illustrates the destructive presence of unmanaged anger:

Matthew and Dee had developed a pattern of interaction in which nearly every conversation was laced with anger, defensiveness, caustic comments, or cynical and sarcastic humor. Ironically, they had a strong foundation and were committed to the relationship but were very tired of the constant presence of anger. Dee has a strong personality and is very outspoken. She was unaware that much of what she said was delivered with an edge and that she was often complaining and accusatory. Matthew is more easy going and reacted to much of what Dee said with defensiveness or humor. He was also passive aggressive and self-absorbed and had developed a pattern over the years of not listening to her. He literally did not hear what she said! After several painful and difficult sessions requiring that they observe their own behavior (self-awareness), practice modifying their own styles of relating (managing and regulating emotion), and approach each other with greater understanding and acceptance (empathy and attunement), things began to shift. Both needed further training in how to respond to and help manage their partner's emotions as well. Because their patterns had been deeply entrenched for many years, permanent change will require consistent, daily effort over an extended period of time.

Stopping the Blame Game

The easiest thing for most of us to do in a conflict or disagreement is to blame the other person. And sometimes the most difficult is to identify and stay focused on our own contribution to a problem. To stop the blame game, it is essential that you work on and focus on your own feelings and behaviors—not on those of your partner.

By remaining attuned, you are less likely to get caught up in blaming each other.

It is exciting to learn to use "preface statements" when you have to discuss tough issues with each other. Using such statements takes the blaming and faultfinding out of your interactions. Prefaces can include such things as those listed below. Keep this list handy and add to it. Try these suggestions with your partner, and keep track of those that work best for you.

- "I have something to talk to you about. Please hear me out and try not to get angry/be hurt/overreact."

- "I know we've discussed this many times, but I feel it is still unsettled and I need to talk about it again."

- "I don't say this to upset you, but I have to talk to you about _____."

- "Are you in the mood to talk about _____ right now?"

- "I know this is a sensitive issue but . . . "

- "Is this a good time to discuss _____?"

- "I'd like to discuss _____ without a lot of anger. Are you willing?"

When you are already in the midst of an argument (and have already used prefaces), you can regroup and salvage things before they escalate. This does require you to be self-aware, positive, and optimistic and to use self-discipline in expressing your feelings—essential EQ qualities for conflict.

- You can stop (in the midst of battle) and say, "May I start over?"

- "Maybe you're right."

- "Please hear me out."

- "Can you speak more softly?"

- "We're both getting angry; can we take a break?"

- "Can we back up and try again?"

- "We're not really getting anywhere with this."

- "I'm not sure we're hearing each other."

I strongly suggest that you put salvaging phrases such as these and the preface statements listed above on 3 x 5 cards and keep them handy or posted in a convenient place for ready access. Try to use them when you and your partner are in conflict and you are tempted to blame or become angry. It takes courage and maturity to change yourself but little skill to insist that your partner change. In most relationships we have to change the way we see our partners. Your partner is not always the problem—your perception may be.

It is important to keep in mind the power of your perceptions. Remember that your beliefs determine what you select to perceive, your beliefs determine your thoughts, both thoughts and perceptions cause you to see what you want to see to validate your beliefs, and you recall and refer to what you find useful to validate your beliefs. Sound circular? It is. See Figure 4-1.

It is not uncommon for the blaming and anger in your relationship to be the result of projecting onto your partner your unfinished or unhealed issues from the past. So when you are tempted to blame, stop and look in the mirror. An interesting aspect of managing conflict is reflected in the following example:

> Margo and Dan rushed into their second marriage too quickly and did not take needed time to heal and become strong individuals between relationships. Margo had come from an emotionally abusive first marriage. She had developed a pattern of being overaccommodating and "people pleasing" in response to her first husband's controlling style and was now projecting residual anger onto Dan. Whenever he asked anything of her, she would accommodate but become furious if he was not grateful or if her own needs were not met. She struggled with a bout of depression, which was likely latent from her first marriage, and would burst into tearful rages, blaming Dan for her unhappiness. Not understanding the effect of her past experience on the present, he would respond angrily and bitter fighting would ensue. Over time, Margo began to recognize that she was projecting her pain onto Dan and blaming him for the hurt she had experienced before entering this marriage. Dan began to recognize an insensitive pattern, which he had modeled after his cold and angry father. They became more attuned to one another, were able to stop the blame game, and learned to manage and express their emotions more appropriately.

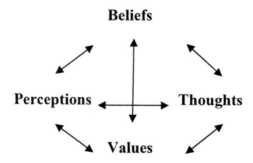

Figure 4-1

Listening Is Loving

There are not as many resources available for learning effective listening as there are for anger management. *The Lost Art of Listening* by Mike Nichols, Ph.D., comprehensively covers many aspects of effective listening. But again, it is a skill that cannot be applied without EQ. The most troublesome obstacle to effective communicating in the face of conflict is the inability or unwillingness to *listen*. Conversely, effective and empathic listening is one of the most powerful forces in making your marriage run smoothly. Remember that what you say may ultimately be less important than what you truly *hear*.

Effective listening skills are a subset of being empathic and attuned to your partner. You may make as many mistakes with your ears, so to speak, as with your tongue in communicating and in conflict. Consider the following guidelines for active and effective listening. Use these guidelines to evaluate yourself as you observe your interactions with your partner. Ask if he/she feels that you have truly heard them when you talk to each other.

- Maintain eye contact, e.g., don't appear distracted.

- Use receptive and open body language, e.g., don't cross your arms or turn away. Lean in and don't move away. Don't pound your fist or stiffen.

- Ask appropriate probing questions—show that you are listening by gathering more information. Questions are extremely important in listening.

- Give only invited and welcome feedback or advice—ask your partner if he/she would be open to your feedback or ideas.

- Get clarity on what they are trying to convey—find a way to make sure you understand what they are saying. Ask questions!

- Remain quietly attentive while you focus on what your partner is saying—be quiet and don't interject your own issues or concerns.

You may want to claim that you can't listen and "think straight" when you are angry and in conflict with your partner or that it is unrealistic to follow the rules of fair fight techniques at these times. This is not true if you can stay tuned in to yourself and your partner, can keep negativity from interfering with your ability to think, and can use your anger adaptively. And emotionally intelligent people can do this!

If your anger has escalated to rage, the situation can be more difficult; however, most interactions do not reach this level. It is precisely when things get heated that fair fight skills and EQ are most needed and can be most useful. As a conflict resolution tool, listening requires maturity, which may be hard to maintain when things get heated.

While it is often in the face of conflict that hostility emerges, respect and a genuine desire for resolution can disarm this hostility. Do you respect your partner? Do you really want to resolve things? Then listen to him/her! The same is true for stubbornness, which can be a positive quality if you use it appropriately as in being resolute or persistent. However, in personal conflict situations it can create a power struggle between you and your partner and make things worse. Again, do you really want to resolve things? Listen. Listening is loving and can break through stubbornness.

Sharing the Problem

Many couples seek help with one in the "complaining" or "unhappy" mode and the other saying, "we are doing fine, we don't need help" or "*you* have a problem, not me." Not the case! If one of you has a concern about your relationship or a concern that affects the relationship, you both have a problem. With a clear explanation, the noncomplaining partner is usually able to see that issues of concern to one of you are shared by both of you.

It is common for us to be fiercely committed to being right and winning arguments. Have you ever found yourself making the claim that you cannot win an argument with your partner? My response to this comment is, tongue in cheek, "Good, I'm glad to hear that." In appropriate conflict management, there is no winner and the disagreement ends with a win-win situation or with an "agree to disagree" arrangement.

Generally speaking, when one person in the relationship has a problem, both do.

Appropriate conflict management usually requires taking ownership and being able to apologize when you have been wrong, hurtful, or out of line. As an antidote to blaming, it clearly requires you to use your emotions appropriately, resist your impulses, be persistent, be tolerant, and delay your own gratification. Tough to do! But emotionally intelligent people can be accountable and do this.

In *How to Say It for Couples*, author Paul Coleman, Psy.D., says, "If you always need to be right in your relationship, you're wrong."[21] The purpose of relationship conflict is to understand your partner's point of view and feelings. It works well if it goes both ways. This concept may be scary to you if it feels like a loss of power and control or that you will never get what you want or need. But if you persist in sharing the problem, you will eventually see its potential for empowerment. You ultimately feel more personally powerful, not less so.

If in the face of conflict you can "partner up" and join each other in a search for an answer or a solution, see yourselves as *we*, and ask questions such as "What can *we* do about this?" or "How can *we* solve this?," a lot of hurt and pain can be avoided. Asking these two questions will help mitigate the majority of conflicts. The conflict itself will not be seen as such a destructive thing. The EQ necessary to do this includes regulating your emotions, being persistent, and controlling your impulses. Your ultimate goal is peaceful coexistence. You can do this!

Incompatibility

When you compare yourself to your partner, you may find the following common differences:

○ **We were raised in different kinds of family systems.**

○ **We have different personalities.**

○ **We have different ways of relating.**

○ **We represent different gender perspectives.**

○ **We are put together differently in our emotional styles.**

○ **We have somewhat different beliefs and values.**

○ **We have different needs.**

○   We express ourselves differently.

○   We like to do things differently.

The "spin" I put on this is that true incompatibility does not really exist in most relationships. It is not specific issues that make or break a relationship but how you talk about them. Problems occur if you lack EQ. It's clearly this lack of EQ and conflict management skills that is the problem, not the "incompatibilities" or presenting issues.

I encourage you to go back and evaluate your level of EQ when you are tempted to claim that you and your partner are incompatible. While this may appear on the surface to be "just plain common sense," a remarkable number of couples insist that the problem with their relationship/marriage is that they are incompatible due to their differences. It can take a great deal of time and effort to see that the *process* of how you handle conflict is far more significant than the *content*.

A Final Word on Conflict

Positive thinking, one of the key EQ skills, is also essential in the face of conflict. Negative thoughts about your partner can have enormous power. If you get stuck on or ruminate about something you dislike in your partner or an action that has upset you instead of limiting these thoughts or replacing them with positive ones, damage may result. Thoughts can be very powerful—whether negative or positive—and can have an immense impact on your interpretation of events and others' actions.

It is best to have many more positive interactions with your partner than negative if you want to have a peaceful relationship/marriage. And this is true for thoughts and feelings as well—it is better to have many more positive thoughts and feelings about your partner than negative. I have witnessed innumerable examples of successful "turnarounds" when couples pause to replace negative actions, thoughts, and feelings with positive ones.

SUMMARY

Nearly all of the characteristics of EQ are required in dealing with the issues discussed in this chapter. This is particularly true of conflict but also applies to honoring needs and respecting differences.

These qualities include:

- Being self-aware and having self-knowledge

- Maintaining enthusiasm and persistence in the face of frustration or setbacks and having the capacity to tolerate defeat

- Delaying gratification and controlling or resisting impulses

- Keeping distress from swamping your ability to think

- Empathizing and being attuned to your partner

- Maintaining hope, positive thinking, and an attitude of optimism

- Regulating or managing your emotions and expressing or using them appropriately

The ability to *control your impulses and delay gratification* is essential in all areas of life—your workplace, social settings, and family—and without it, chaos would reign. This is particularly key in maintaining a healthy relationship, especially when you are facing conflict. The temptation to verbally lash out and be hurtful, to be defensive, to lay blame on your partner, or to act in destructive ways is particularly strong when you are angry. If you lack impulse control, you are at great risk in your relationship; this situation is made worse when you are also unable to delay gratification or unable to be *persistent when frustrated*. Lacking these qualities can lead to actions you often later regret.

Modern living exposes us to many situations, both personal and professional, which cause us great distress. At those times our ability to think straight can be compromised. It is perhaps in the face of conflict or when we are angry that we are at greatest risk. Thus, it is important to have the ability to *keep distress from swamping our ability to think* and to *override negative emotions* to perform (and relate) effectively. It is not necessarily "oxymoronic" to think straight in the midst of anger or conflict. An emotionally intelligent person can do this.

The ability to think straight is akin to a similar EQ quality—that of actually using your moods or emotions for adaptive and constructive behaviors. This is reflected in the commonly heard statement, "When I am upset, I throw myself into my work" or " I clean my house like crazy when I'm mad." There are a number of ways to use your emotions constructively. In your personal interactions, to be able to calm down and help your partner calm down is most helpful and requires the ability, once again, to *be empathetic and tuned in* to both your own and your partner's emotions.

To develop and apply these skills, you must be able to self-monitor and have *self-awareness*. You cannot master *impulse control, delay gratification*, deal with frustration, override distress, or use your emotions effectively if you are not aware of your motivations and feelings or are unable to control your behaviors. This requires an ability to "check into yourself" and carry on appropriate self-dialogue about how to respond during difficult times.

In addition to conflict management, an equally helpful ability is that of identifying your needs and feelings and expressing them to your partner. This is part of being *self-aware and self-knowledgeable*, and it can prevent disaster. Perhaps you get frustrated or hurt when your needs are not met by your partner or your feelings are not acknowledged. However, to have them honored, your needs and feelings should be clearly "published" to your partner. Hopefully he/she is emotionally intelligent enough to be receptive and to really listen to you. Your partner should not be expected to read your mind.

Once expressed by yourself and understood by your partner, needs are more likely to be met, feelings respected, and beliefs honored. Likewise, if you expect your partner to "open up" and share his/her needs or feelings, you must be able to *empathize and be attuned* to them and receptive to whatever they are sharing.

Sometimes the ability to delay gratification is called for if there is a clash of needs (I call it a "needs contest"), and one of you may have to set aside your needs temporarily to meet those of your partner. This can be an emotionally intelligent response as long as there is balance and "taking turns." Deferring too often or, conversely, dominating and insisting upon getting your way is likely to eventually lead to decay in your relationship.

The respect for and tolerance of your differences requires some of the same EQ qualities that are needed for conflict management. Having differences is inevitable, and if they are substantial, not knowing how to handle them can lead to unnecessary hurt and frustration. Dealing with a partner who is quite different from you requires an ability to maintain an enthusiastic attitude despite frustration and viewing the differences as a positive thing and with an attitude of optimism. As with all relationship issues, you have to remain self-aware and focus on being empathetic and attuned to your partner.

• • •

Congratulations! You have worked through some of the most challenging aspects of a committed love relationship. Part II (Chapters 5 through 7) provides a shift in our focus. I will take you through three issues that you will not find discussed in most other books for couples. Chapter 5 shows you how EQ is required for your self-esteem and how this affects your relationship.

PART II

CHAPTER FIVE

Self-Esteem

Can I Love You if I Don't Love Me?

The glory is not in never failing,
but in rising every time you fail.

—CHINESE PROVERB

Your self-esteem and perception of yourself have a significant impact on your relationship/marriage. In this chapter we begin by defining terms and talking about how self-esteem is formed. Then the role it plays in your relationship and how maintaining it requires emotional intelligence (EQ) is addressed.

WHAT IS SELF-ESTEEM?

It is your honest evaluation of yourself. Over time I have come to see the importance of differentiating among self-concept, self-confidence (which includes self-efficacy), and self-love, all of which contribute to your self-esteem. Although these overlap, let's take a quick look at each.

Your self-concept is generally an objective view of what you perceive as your personal characteristics and the kind of person you see yourself being. Self-esteem is a subjective evaluation or judgment of whether you like or approve of yourself. For example, I may recognize that I am a shy and quiet person. That is my self-concept. My self-esteem is reflected in the degree to which I approve or like this about myself. Is it OK with me that I am shy and quiet?

Self-concept is a relatively judgment-free description of yourself, i.e., "I am outgoing," "I am overweight," "I am a spiritual person," "I flunked out of college," "I am divorced." Your self-concept can be sabotaged by judging yourself too harshly. What turns an objective reality into a value-laden subjective view is your self-esteem. "I flunked out of college" can be changed from a simple fact to " . . . because I am stupid or a loser." Or "I am divorced" can become "I am a failure at relationships." Or to use a positive example, "I am outgoing" can be seen as "I am well liked and successful because I am outgoing."

Self-confidence is one aspect of your self-esteem that involves ego strength and courage. It reflects an attitude of "I can do it" or "I will try to do it" despite obstacles or shortcomings. This overlaps with but is not entirely the same as the EQ quality of self-efficacy. Confidence is a crucial ingredient in the success of your relationship.

If you want to be mentally healthy (and who doesn't?), you can learn to shape your reality in a direction that builds your self-esteem, gives you a belief in your personal efficacy, and helps you have an optimistic view of your future.

Self-efficacy, a component of both self-esteem and EQ, is the belief in and ability to use your resources under all circumstances, including the most difficult. In other words, if you are a self-efficacious person, you will have a sense of personal power and know that you have an effect on outcomes and circumstances in your life no matter what. You don't get caught in a "victim mentality" or the belief that the world is out to get you when things go wrong.

You may have heard about "locus of control," which also has to do with your belief about how much control you have over what happens to you in life. At one extreme you may believe everything that occurs in your life is the result of

Self-efficacy and self-confidence can make all the difference between success and failure in life.

your own actions and attributes. Or you may believe that what happens to you is the result of forces beyond your control. Most of us are somewhere in the middle, and neither extreme is particularly functional. However, if you lean toward an internal orientation, you are more likely to have higher self-esteem, self-efficacy, and self-motivation. If you have a more external locus of control, this is less likely.

Self-love is that aspect of your self-esteem that runs much deeper into your psyche and shows respect for and appreciation of your essence or core self. It is not dependent upon your competence, behaviors, failures or successes, personal traits, talents, appearance, and the like. Some well-known people in the public eye who appear to have great ego strength and high self-esteem candidly carry deep self-doubt, and they struggle with true self-acceptance or self-love.

Your level of self-love or lack thereof is rooted in your early developmental years and can be improved through learning, healing, and effort. Self-love can be considered the spiritual component of your self-esteem. If you have developed a mature spirituality, you are more likely to experience self-love than someone who has not. This is based on your belief that you are unconditionally loved and accepted by God or your concept of a universal power.

HOW IS SELF-ESTEEM FORMED?

Most experts agree that self-esteem is primarily formed during the early years of your life. Your sense of self and self-esteem are the result of social and environmental influences, but they are not cast in impermeable stone and can be modified even now. The EQ qualities that can help improve your self-esteem are being self-aware, having the ability to maintain enthusiasm and persistence when facing frustration, having the capacity to tolerate defeat, being hopeful and optimistic, and being self-motivated.

While your external influences are extremely powerful, you also have some power and autonomy in all of this. Richard Bednar, Ph.D., and Scott Peterson in their *Self-esteem: Paradoxes and Innovations in Clinical Theory and Practice* tell us something very important: "Children who are so lucky as to have affirming, affectionate, and loving parents should have unquestioning self-confidence. Conversely, children whose parents were harsh and critical should inexorably be victims who gradually internalize the criticisms as the given definition of themselves. Yet our clinical experience has taught us that this is not always the case. Some individuals coming from an abusive and/or traumatic childhood are remarkably intact, productive, and self-confident. Others, who come from apparently nurturing supportive environments, may or may not be equally productive and suffer from debilitating self-doubt and low self-esteem."[22]

You can learn self-affirmation if you received negative messages about yourself or had ego-bruising experiences. Early influences can be overcome, although it is a real challenge for most of us, which requires that we manage our emotions and be persistent. You may have to work hard to feel better about yourself and love yourself more. That's OK! Better to work at it than to live unfulfilled.

You can transform your life. The way you feel about yourself affects your behaviors, choices, decisions, and all aspects of your life, including your love relationship. Nathaniel Branden, Ph.D., well known for his work in self-esteem, says that real self-esteem also includes personal responsibility and conscious living.

"If we are not at war with ourselves, we are less likely to be at war with others."

—Nathaniel Branden, Ph.D.

Use the following list to evaluate your own level of personal responsibility and conscious living. Do you need to work on any of these issues? Do you see how they might affect your interactions with your partner?

- Considering the rights and feelings of others

- Seeing yourself and others realistically

- Making conscious choices

- Choosing clarity over confusion

- Maintaining self–awareness (of your thoughts, feelings, and actions)

- Acting in accordance with what you see and know

- Avoiding denial or a victim mentality

- Living in the present

- Paying attention to your inner signals

- Living actively not passively

SELF-ESTEEM AND COMMITTED RELATIONSHIPS

Self-esteem works both ways for couples—it can either be damaged by one or both of you or it can be enhanced by your interactions.

While the approval or praise of your love partner does not create or sustain your self-esteem, he/she does have a responsibility to support your growth and treat you with respect and dignity. Have you noticed that you feel better about yourself when you treat your partner with dignity, listen to them carefully, believe in them, acknowledge their resources, and see beyond the surface to their deeper value? When you live from the best within yourself, you will draw out the best in your partner. Your own self-esteem as well as that of your partner is best served when you interact lovingly.

You can be loving by being tuned in to your loved one, which means being aware of their feelings and needs. It also means you will be compassionate toward them. If your self-esteem is fairly solid, you are likely to treat your partner with respect. That arrogant, puffed-up, self-absorbed person you see at work, in social situations, and possibly in your family is probably low in self-esteem and has problems relating to others. Likewise, the individual who is defensive, critical, and judgmental of others is probably trying to hide their own self-doubt.

It doesn't take a very close examination to recognize that this corresponds with various aspects of EQ. The more you like and respect yourself, the less likely you are to find fault with others and blame them for your problems or unhappiness. And this includes your partner!

You can love yourself when you see yourself accurately, appreciate what you see, and are excited about the prospect of who you can become.

Have you ever heard anyone say, "You can't love another person unless you love yourself?" What about "It's difficult to love someone who doesn't love themselves?" These may be popular catchy phrases, but there is some conventional wisdom here.

It works like this: If you are excessively needy and insecure, it can be difficult for your partner to maintain respect for you. Mutual respect is fundamental to a firm foundation for most couples. An insecure or needy person begins to feel like a burden—an albatross—to the other.

Remember that we are focusing on a healthy relationship. Some people initially prefer insecure partners or those with low self-esteem because this allows them to be superior and/or in the role of caretaker or controller. This is obviously not a picture of a healthy relationship.

This story demonstrates the role of self-esteem in marriage:

John and Lisa had been married for nearly ten years and had two young sons. When I began my work with them, John was devoid of EQ and was psychologically unsophisticated. He had little self-knowledge, communicated poorly, was defensive when asked questions about himself, could not identify or report his feelings, became discouraged easily, was quite negative about himself and life in general, and had difficulty tuning in to others. An assessment did not reveal depression, but he clearly had low self-esteem, which negatively impacted their marriage. Lisa wanted John to be decisive so that she did not have to make all the decisions, but he routinely deferred to her. When he did make a decision, he did so in a controlling, noninclusive way, which is common among individuals who do not feel a sense of their own personal power.

Whenever John had a difficult time or was upset, he blamed himself and could not objectively problem solve with her, berating himself instead of focusing on the issue at hand. He relied on her to support and encourage him; however, when she suffered a bout of depression, he had a difficult time reciprocating. John's body image was poor, his friends were few, and Lisa could not maintain the level of respect she desired to have for her husband. This was a difficult case to treat because his motivation to learn about himself and engage in personal growth was minimal. However, his desire to keep his marriage intact provided the impetus to move forward. Eventually, John began to assert himself and his needs appropriately, began a fitness program to enhance his body image, took a greater leadership role in their family, and his self-esteem inched forward. At the time of this writing he still had a long way to go, but Lisa reports that as his level of respect for himself is increasing, he feels less like an albatross and more like a partner.

We all have insecurities; however, if you have too many, you have less upon which to draw in giving love to your partner. You may express your love in a needy "please love me" or "please don't leave me" style but may not be capable of the demands of mature love. In short, to be loved and to give love in a mature way is more difficult if you struggle excessively with your self-esteem.

Many of us began our relationship or marriage in an immature and needy state whether we knew it or not. Some common issues reflecting low levels of self-esteem or too much neediness are listed below. Do you or your partner show these signs of insecurity?

- **Defensiveness**
- **Jealousy**
- **Possessiveness**
- **Unwillingness to be held accountable**
- **Attitude of blaming**
- **Competitiveness**
- **Inability to give and receive love and affection in a mature way**
- **Passiveness**
- **Erratic emotionality**
- **Need for control**
- **Desire to win**

While any of these could be a symptom of something else, they all show a lack of EQ.

Our culture promotes the notion, both subtly and directly, that you must please others to be accepted, must look to others for praise and positive feedback, and can find happiness by finding a partner or marrying. Your sense of self and happiness should not come solely from your partner. Expecting him/her to be your primary or sole source of happiness or self-esteem is quite common; but it puts an enormous burden on your partner and strains your relationship. This was reinforced for me in a recent conversation with a client who said that the only thing that gave his life meaning and made him happy was being with his girlfriend. Think about that.

Quite naturally, your self-esteem is partially enhanced by positive feedback, and part of your role in a relationship is to support, stroke, and help build up your partner. If you are mature and emotionally intelligent, you can be supportive, sensitive, and empathic to your mate while at the same time maintaining responsibility for your own happiness and well-being. Your self-esteem is an internal process that focuses on self-evaluations and carefully observing yourself (self-awareness). It is not overly dependent on others' approval.

The more you understand yourself (self-awareness) and maintain a realistic self-appreciation and self-respect, the more likely you are to give to and receive from your partner. Your self-esteem may increase as a result of the love and support of your partner, but it cannot be sustained if it is built on this alone.

Autonomy

While it is a major life goal for most of us to be part of a committed partnership, you have to first be autonomous, alone, and individuated. A healthy and balanced person is able to have close, personal, or committed relationships but also has the capacity to maintain individuality and be comfortable with aloneness. This is extremely important.

You may not be responsible for your partner's self-esteem, but you can contribute to enhancing or diminishing it over time. One way to do this is to be supportive of his/her autonomy or self-determination.

Supporting your partner's autonomy involves:

- **Respecting your partner's point of view**

- **Encouraging choice and initiative**

- Communicating in a noncontrolling way

- Offering positive feedback

- Allowing "space" or time alone for his/her personal interests and pursuits

Supporting your partner's autonomy can be complicated if you are not truly attuned to the needs and feelings of your partner. Using the list above as a self-test, ask yourself if you support your partner's autonomy.

If your relationship creates an autonomy-supporting environment, you and your partner are likely to:

- Achieve more

- See yourselves as more competent

- Be more flexible in your thinking

- Get pleasure from optimal challenges

- Have more positive, personal, and emotional exchanges

- Trust each other more

- Make and maintain behavioral changes

To do this, you have to use your EQ: be self-motivated, be able to manage your emotions, be persistent, understand yourself, and be empathic with your partner. Use the checklist above after you and your partner have consciously worked at supporting each other's autonomy for a while, perhaps several weeks. Any progress?

Chances are you have seen a couple in which one or the other was overly controlling or bossy. This "micromanaging" can be stifling to the growth, esteem, and initiative of the other person. (This is, by the way, a common parenting style as well.) Why should you attempt to make decisions, take action, or achieve anything if the person you are with is hovering about telling you what and how to think, feel, and act? Conversely, what a growth-producing gift you can give to each other in a relationship—an autonomy-supporting attitude and environment.

Inevitably, there is some loss of autonomy in all relationships, especially if you have been together for several years. There is some degree of blurring of boundaries, blending of egos, and loss of individuality. In the past, this blurring was seen by some as a sign of a good marriage. After all, the traditional wedding vows include the phrase "and the two shall become as one." We are now able to recognize the potential danger in this blending and the potential loss of autonomy to which it can lead.

This example illustrates the danger of not maintaining your autonomy in a marriage:

> Most individuals whose self-esteem and autonomy are overly dependent upon their partners and rooted in their relationship lack an awareness of this pattern. Often it is only when the relationship begins to unravel that this dependence becomes apparent. This couple's experience demonstrates this. After a 10-year marriage Doreen and her husband, James, separated. During a long separation and the impending completion of divorce Doreen began to see that she had not really maintained as strong a sense of self and autonomy as she had heretofore believed. It became apparent that she had allowed her motivation for any of her accomplishments or successes to be based on James' approval and his high energy level to energize her. She was a person with a low energy level, and his disapproval of her influenced much of her behavior.

Again, while this may not be uncommon in long-term marriages, this realization was extremely painful for Doreen. She had convinced herself that she really was a self-motivated and strong individual throughout the marriage. After hanging onto and maintaining contact with each other throughout their separation, divorce became inevitable; Doreen had to face the reality of moving forward on her own. At the time of this writing she is engaged in a process of trying to establish a sense of self and greater autonomy, perhaps for the first time in her life.

Emotion and Self-Esteem

The maintenance of self-esteem depends on your ability to identify and appropriately use your emotions. While cognitive awareness or knowledge of your abilities and good qualities may be somewhat helpful in maintaining self-confidence, it is fundamentally how you feel about yourself that really determines your self-esteem.

Consider this—let's assume you are an individual with low self-esteem who believes that you need a great deal of stroking and positive feedback or reassurances of undying love from your partner. If they comply and present you with many compliments and reassurances based on objective fact as they believe it, you may discount this because you do not feel the truth of what is being offered. You cannot accept this at an emotional level. Your partner, who is attempting to bolster you, will eventually give up with a "why bother" attitude. Your neediness can weigh heavily on your partner and can be a real "turn off." This is an example of the view mentioned earlier—it is difficult to love someone if they don't love themselves.

Conversely, if you have a strong sense of self and your partner attempts for whatever reason to denigrate or lower that esteem, you will not be convinced of the credibility of his/her "put downs" because you have, at a feeling or emotional level, an enduring sense of self-approval.

Yes, your cognitive processes or the way you think does play an important role in the establishment and maintenance of your self-esteem. However, it is at a feeling level that self-esteem is more enduring and unshakable—either positively or negatively " . . . we consider emotions to be the crowning element in the development of either high or low levels of self-esteem . . . Self-esteem is not a thought but a subjective and enduring state of realistic self-approval. It is a feeling people experience about themselves . . . The development of self-esteem is directly anchored to what people actually experience affectively (at a feeling level) about themselves."[23]

This also applies to how you feel about life in general. People with low self-esteem are more prone to negative emotions such as anger and depression as well as pessimism in general. Your negative thoughts and feelings have a profound impact on your relationship. This is when the EQ quality of being positive and hopeful can be useful. Your feelings in general, not just your feelings about yourself, clearly impact the health and functioning of your relationship.

In some cases self-esteem is not cause but effect. For example, having strong self-esteem may not cause you to succeed but be the result of being successful at something. This dovetails with the idea that your self-esteem is feeling based and may therefore be affected by your successes and relationships in life. This then underscores the necessity for EQ in your relationship—if you can maintain emotional equilibrium in your interactions with a significant other, the stability of your self-esteem is more likely to be ensured and under your control. The process is somewhat paradoxical: you are responsible for your sense of self but, because you are a feeling-based human being, you are also vulnerable to the views of and treatment by others. The greater your EQ, the more you can maintain equilibrium in this pull between yourself and your partner.

The following example illustrates the potential vulnerability of one's self-esteem to the treatment by others close to us:

In some cases low self-esteem leads to the choice of a partner who reinforces one's worthlessness. Such was the case with Beth. She grew up with an abusive, alcoholic father and a neglectful mother, choosing to marry in her late teens in a search for love. Unfortunately, her husband, Joe, was a very troubled, abusive young man who died at a young age. Beth continued a pattern of subsequent relationships with abusive partners, heavy drinking, and self-loathing. When I met Beth, she was emotionally unstable and devastated by the ending of her most recent unhealthy relationship but clinging to it for her sense of worth. At the time of this writing she was in the process of healing from unmet needs in her family of origin and slowly rebuilding a stronger sense of self in the hope that she can someday maintain a relationship with a partner who does not reinforce her worthlessness. Beth is an inherently bright and competent person who is gradually learning to manage her emotions and is developing the qualities of EQ that will ideally allow for both personal and relational fulfillment.

What follows is a list of characteristics common in people with strong self-esteem. Note that many of these are also qualities reflecting EQ in general. Individuals with good self-esteem:

- Feel confident in most situations.

- Are comfortable being alone.

- Are not overly dependent upon others.

- Are hopeful and optimistic.

- Live an active not passive life.

- Are congruent in words and actions.

- Take care of their bodies.

- Can identify and express their needs.

- Can identify and express their feelings.

- Are capable of experiencing intimacy.

- Avoid people pleasing and caretaking.

- Know and use their personal power.

- Are honest with themselves.

- Are able to be playful and spontaneous.

- Experience joy in life.

- Can relate to their "inner selves."

- Are open to feedback and criticism.

- Are productive.

- Use their talents.

- Can identify and correct their mistakes.

- Are benevolent and respectful.

- Take appropriate risks.

- Promote others' growth and self-esteem.

- Enjoy the successes of others.

- Accept people for who they are.

- Are compassionate but avoid pitying.

- Are able to forgive.

- Accept compliments comfortably.

- Have the ability to fulfill themselves in life.

- Are not critical or judgmental of others.

If you would like to evaluate your level of self-esteem as it relates to your love relationship and your EQ, see Appendix B.

SUMMARY

While nearly all of the characteristics of EQ can be applied to the effect of self-esteem in your relationship, I propose that the following six are most essential:

1. Being self-aware and having self-knowledge

2. Being self-motivated—managing your emotions to reach a goal

3. Maintaining enthusiasm and persistence in the face of frustration or setbacks and having the capacity to tolerate defeat

4. Maintaining a sense of self-efficacy

5. Maintaining hope, positive thinking, and an attitude of optimism

6. Empathizing and being attuned to others, especially your partner, and dealing with them effectively

It is often said that "the most successful people are those who know how to fail." Some of the world's most successful or accomplished people have an ongoing battle with maintaining genuine self-esteem. Self-esteem is maintained by *self-motivation*, an ability to *manage your emotions* to stay focused, a sustained *enthusiasm in the face of frustration*, and an ability to *tolerate defeat*. If your tendency is to give up easily, you can expect this to have an adverse effect on your relationship. You only have to think for a moment to see how often these EQ qualities apply to your interactions with your partner.

These EQ qualities are even more important if, as suggested in this chapter, you were not encouraged, or conversely, were criticized and discouraged a great deal in your early years. But success breeds success, and the more you can develop these qualities and overcome present and past obstacles, the stronger you become. Self-esteem and certain characteristics of EQ work in a circular way—each enhancing the other.

All of these qualities are built upon the belief that you have some power over outcomes in your life and that you can have an effect on the results of your efforts. This *self-efficacious attitude* results from self-confidence and at the same time helps to create it. This then is the opposite of a "victim" mentality and leads to greater individual autonomy.

And what could be more important in maintaining self-esteem than a *positive, hopeful, optimistic* attitude? You are bombarded daily with experiences and messages in your life and relationships that could interfere with your self-love, damage your self-esteem, and lower your self-confidence. Some days it takes a Herculean effort to continue to move forward, believe in yourself, and hang on to the belief that all will ultimately be well. But without this belief that there is always *hope* and without the ability to reframe things from a *positive* perspective, you are likely to slip into fear, lose your footing, and develop self-doubt.

Can you be self-confident and self-loving and maintain high self-esteem if you do not truly know or *understand yourself?* Without this comprehension, your sense of self is likely to be superficial and vulnerable to outside influences. You may appear confident in a transparent or arrogant way. Genuine *self-awareness* and *self-knowledge* help you know who you truly are, what you feel, what your beliefs are, and as much as possible how you present yourself and come across to others. In a relationship, if you truly know yourself and feel confident in who you are, this makes you much less vulnerable to the inevitable slights and hurtful things that come with being part of a couple. You will be much better at weathering "relationship storms."

It is also necessary to be truly *attuned to* and have compassion for your partner to support his/her self-esteem. Ask yourself, Can I really love, respect, and appreciate you at any level of depth if I don't truly know you or am not attuned to you and feel empathy for you?

A final word—some individuals are supremely confident and have high self-esteem only within their area of comfort. If you have the ability to *maintain enthusiasm and persistence in the face of frustration*, you can use this in most settings or circumstances even if you are outside your "comfort zone." Genuine self-esteem helps you face new or difficult challenges, including the doubts of or devaluing by your partner and the unfamiliar or taxing experiences that come with a relationship/marriage. It can be very empowering.

• • •

It is hardly appropriate to call the mind–body–spirit paradigm "new." You have heard a lot about it in recent years. But can you really explain how your mind affects your body and vice versa? Or how your spirit interacts with each of these? Now let's move on to Chapter 6 and take a look at what this triad has to do with EQ and love relationships.

CHAPTER SIX

The Mind–Body Connection
Health and Fitness in Relationships

So many of our dreams at first seem impossible,
then they seem improbable, and then, when we
summon the will, they soon become inevitable.

—CHRISTOPHER REEVE

I t is no longer disputable that as you experience changes in your mind, you experience changes in your body or biology. The brain's activity in your mind sets the stage for your behavior as well as defending against illness and promoting health and well-being—the mind–body connection. The im-

The benefits of fitness and good physical health include improved mental health, potential for increased EQ, and improvement in the quality of your close relationships.

portant intangibles in your life such as your thoughts, feelings, motivations, and beliefs are always the result of chemical and electrical activity in the nerve cells in your body and brain. And all of these determine how you function in your relationship.

A BRIEF REVIEW OF THE MIND–BODY–SPIRIT PARADIGM

Within recent years there has been an information explosion about the connections among our emotions, health, and spirit. But the notion that our mind, body, and spirit are interconnected is rooted in history.

As far back as the first century Hippocrates, often credited as the "father of medicine," introduced the notion of the interaction between our bodily fluids or "humors" and our personality characteristics and emotional states. Certain imbalances in these fluids were seen to influence our feelings, personal styles, and disease or illness.

In the psychology and medical fields Figure 6-1 is known as the "biopsychosocial" model for health care. Our culture encourages us to follow lowfat, low-carb, low-salt, or low-calorie diets; lower our cholesterol levels; quit smoking; exercise more; reduce our stress; engage in personal growth; and even deepen our spirituality.

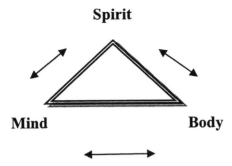

Figure 6-1

If you pick up a popular magazine or watch TV, you will be faced with a story or article regarding some aspect of health or fitness, either emotional or physical—from "Oprah" to "The Today Show"—from NPR to the *New York Times*—from *Sports Illustrated* to *Newsweek*.

Likewise, the presence of spas, gyms, health clubs, health food stores, "natural" grocery markets, sports equipment outlets, weight-loss clinics, races, and marathons all represent numerous opportunities for health and fitness.

Even prominent and established universities offer courses/conferences on the mind–body–spirit interactions to students in the social and psychological sciences as well as in religion and medicine. Examples of this include a course on "Spirituality and Medicine" at the University of Texas Southwestern Medical School and conferences held at Harvard Medical School on "Spirituality and Health." Even The National Institutes of Health spend millions on mind–body medicine.

Is this a fleeting trend or is it a long-overdue recognition of the holistic nature of the human experience? Evidence supports the latter. It is being widely expected by both the scientific world, which does the research, and the general public, which benefits from these findings.

THE FOUNDATION

The early "founding fathers" of psychology, including Freud and Jung, provided numerous examples of the interaction among the psyche or mind, the physiological processes of the body, and the spirit dimension. They laid valuable groundwork for current research efforts and treatment techniques.

Bernie Siegel, M.D., in his best seller, *Love, Medicine, and Miracles*, describes how patient after patient have found the power of laughter and humor in a loving, safe, and supportive environment to be both healing and sustaining. The catecholamines in the brain (chemicals usually associated with response to stress or emergencies) have been found to be stimulated by humor, and they relieved pain in his patients, who were amused and laughed a great deal.

Another pioneer of the current mind–body perspective was Norman Cousins, a University of California at Los Angeles professor and popular author. Cousins, who was the originator of the now-popular phrase "belief becomes biology," is well known for his contribution to our awareness that the mind and body are intricately connected and that your frame of mind has a powerful impact on your physical health and well-being. Positive attitudes and emotions and maintaining a sense of hope affect your body's biochemistry and can contribute to your health and rejuvenation. Emotional intelligence (EQ)!

In Anatomy of an Illness, Norman Cousins launched a movement in this culture which has touched the lives of millions and is still unfolding.

How does this relate to your marriage/relationship? The new fields of psychoimmunology and psychoneuroimmunology study the link between your mind and endocrine and immune systems. These and the new medical fields associated with psychology (psychobiology, psychophysiology, and psychospirituality) help us understand EQ, which contributes to healthy love relationships.

Changing thoughts imply a changing brain and thus a changing biology and body.

Salovey, one of the originators of the concept of EQ, says that your emotions are often influenced by your physiological functioning. Your negative emotions and moods can lead to ill health and your positive emotional states to healthier patterns. Even personality styles such as pessimism can increase your susceptibility to illness, while optimistic styles can increase or strengthen your resistance to disease and sickness.

A word of caution: There is no guarantee that by being positive, upbeat, and optimistic, you will not have any health problems or that you are to blame for any illness because you were "not positive enough." Reason must prevail here.

Many of us experience negative emotions because of traumatic life events outside of our control. These must be faced and worked through not denied in an effort to be positive or they will do further damage to your mental

It is not just your emotions or feelings that are associated with health outcomes but your thoughts or cognitive processes as well.

and physical health. But if you can regulate or manage your emotions and maintain a sense of self-efficacy, you can generally recover more quickly.

Your thinking has as much of an impact on your health as your feelings. Toxicity or negative emotions and thoughts both take a toll on physical and mental health and can disrupt your life, including your relationship. Depression, isolation, and loneliness can lead to our most deadly diseases.

Positive or optimistic thinking (not just feelings) can contribute to good health. If you are reactive and defensive, you are more likely to have health problems.

APPLICATION TO YOUR RELATIONSHIPS

Let's take a look at the benefits of good relationships. The positive influence of personal relationships can come from your friends, family, neighbors, coworkers, church community, clubs, or close love relationships or marriage. When you do not have enough psychosocial support, you are more likely to react to stress by getting sick or depressed than when this support is consistent.

As this applies to your love relationship, if you can be truly attuned to your partner and are empathic with him/her, you contribute to his/her health. What a gift!

Here's an ironic twist. If you are consistently negative or sick, people are less drawn to you or less likely to offer you support or help. If you have a more positive attitude or outlook, this is more likely to attract others, including your partner. Appropriate social contact helps you feel positive about yourself, can motivate you to take care of yourself, and can increase your resilience in facing difficulties.

Interpersonal support is healing and preventative because it lowers your emotional defenses, which cause depression and isolation, both of which can sap your physical health.

When your social ties are broken, your immune system is often weakened. Marriage should be a close, intact relationship, and the vulnerability of your immune system can increase if you lose this connection. This is obvious when you look at what happens during and after divorce or the ending of a long-term relationship.

Are you healthier if you are married and less healthy if you are single? This depends on several factors, including whether you have a healthy lifestyle and often times on your level of commitment to fitness. A common complaint from couples is that one partner is too inactive, a "couch potato," and not willing to participate in fitness or athletic activities. This is true of both men and women of all ages.

The feeling of security that comes from knowing help, if needed, is available from social relationships may increase your resilience to both mental and physical illnesses.

It would be naive and ill advised to say that good health is the key factor in making your relationship strong and functional. One or both of you may be in ill health that is beyond your control, but your relationship can remain healthy and satisfying. However, it is true that certain psychological and physical illnesses interfere with activity levels, diet, healthy living, and motivation. No matter what your condition or situation, it is important to be informed about the mind–body connection; everyone benefits from a healthier, more active lifestyle.

The following is a powerful example of overcoming a serious health problem:

I recently learned of a woman who lost both of her hands and all fingers except for a thumb as well as both of her lower legs and feet to a zoophagous (flesh-eating) disease. Despite her losses and limitations, she chose to lead an active and healthy lifestyle. She continues in her career as a successful business woman and maintains a healthy marriage. She is a high-energy, optimistic, independent woman. Perhaps we all know of someone who lives with circumstances reminiscent of what I call "Christopher Reeve's" syndrome. With effective professional help and adequate social and medical support, most of us can choose an active and healthy lifestyle, increasing the chances of a more satisfying life and more fulfilling relationship/marriage.

A caveat: There are couples who choose an unhealthy lifestyle and reject the idea that physical fitness can be of value to them but who nonetheless maintain happy relationships. Likewise, there are those couples who are committed to health and fitness but are miserable together. The bottom line is that optimal health is clearly an asset to you as an individual! In most cases optimal health will therefore contribute to improvement in your interactions with your partner.

Physical and mental health can contribute to your EQ and vice versa. This includes being empathic and tuned in, being hopeful and positive, self-awareness, maintaining enthusiasm and persistence despite defeat, a sense of self-efficacy, delaying gratification,

With adequate social and medical support, most of us can choose an active and healthy lifestyle, increasing the chances of a more satisfying life and more fulfilling relationship.

and self-motivation. You are probably starting to see the connection of how these attributes can improve your relationship.

If you were asked what you value most, would you say that your health and family relationships are your two "most precious possessions"? Would you agree that your life is better when you are in good health? If you are both mentally and physically healthy, you are more likely to be emotionally intelligent, and this may help your relationship/marriage flow and function more smoothly. This "cause and effect" is demonstrated in Figure 6-2.

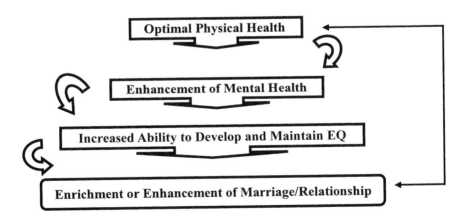

Figure 6-2

It is particularly important to understand the mind–body connection if one or both of you have suffered severe trauma, especially in childhood. This trauma is "locked into" your body and plays a major role in your functioning, including your close interactions. But even if you are a trauma survivor, committing to physical health and fitness can improve your mental health and your relationship.

STRESS

Stress probably best demonstrates the connection between your mind and body. Your love relationship or marriage is inevitably stressful at times, and conversely, the stresses in your own personal life are carried over into your interactions with your partner.

Couples who have chronic patterns of conflict in their relationships have elevated levels of stress hormones (cortisol) as well. It is not your relationship itself but the quality of it that is the predictor of stress and its subsequent effect on your health and wellness.

Stress is both brought into marriage and created by it.

Physiologist Hans Selye, M.D., introduced his innovative general adaptation syndrome theory on stress in the late 1940s. His theory laid the foundation for our understanding of what is now called a psychobiological (mind–body) reaction to things you experience as stressful.

Physical or biological stress can lead to psychological symptoms, and conversely, psychological stress can result in physical symptoms. Many illnesses have a psychosomatic origin.

While stress can result in both psychological and physical symptoms, it is your attitude or cognitive evaluation of your stressors that really makes the difference. In other words, how you interpret what happens to you has much more power or impact than a stressful incident or situation itself. Your body responds to the messages from your brain and not just to what is occurring in your environment.

Helplessness or negative reactions and interpretations of events vs. hopeful and positive ones result in opposite effects on us.

How does EQ fit into this picture? Invaluable in the face of stressors of any kind are the abilities to be persistent, believe that you and/or your partner have some power over what you are facing (self-efficacy), have a hopeful and positive attitude, and are compassionate and empathic with each other (aspects of attunement).

Your level of EQ can help you develop coping skills as well. Believing that you have the skills to cope (an aspect of self-efficacy) is more important than your actual skill level, and this belief has a positive effect on your relationship.

THE BUILDING BLOCKS

The impact of positive and optimistic thinking and attitudes are often compared with those that are negative and pessimistic. A concerted and consistent effort to maintain a positive view of your life's circumstances is more likely to lead to good health, a health-enhancing lifestyle, and a better love relationship.

This positive and optimistic attitude is intensified by the most important elements in maintaining good physical health:

- **Adequate sleep**

- **Proper nutrition**

- **Consistent exercise**

- **Weight management**

As you proceed, remember that it is wise to be well informed or under the care or guidance of someone who has expertise when dealing with your personal health.

Let's take a brief look at these "building blocks" and how they can help you have a healthier relationship as well.

Why do some of us refuse to do what it takes to be healthy and fit? It may appear to be laziness (and some of us may be lazy), but the reasons are more complex. If you are down, unhappy, or negative, you are less likely to believe that there is anything you can do to make yourself healthier. You may focus more on ill health and symptoms, seeking constant medical attention. If you maintain a positive mood or attitude, you are more likely to have health-promoting behaviors and less likely to focus on physical distress or symptoms.

Having a consistent negative mood can lead you to believe that your environment or world is not safe and that there is not much you can do about it. If your partner has this belief and mood state, it can feel suffocating to you.

Mood states can play a significant role in participating in self-care.

The positive perspective says that life is safe and manageable and that there is something you can do to make yourself feel better. Likewise, the belief that you have the ability to control your own life, or self-efficacy, can lead to confidence, which will benefit both of you.

If you are someone who is committed to the health-promoting "building blocks," you know that it is often difficult to stick with them. Being optimistic about future results or benefits can help you remain resilient and persistent. Persistence and resilience are essential EQ ingredients because this lifestyle has to be consistent and lifelong, not a hit and miss process. Yes, it takes EQ to be healthy!

Optimism has numerous benefits for coping, stress management, recovery from health problems, and overall well-being.

What follows is an explanation of the benefits of each of the building blocks, how they require EQ, and how developing them will enhance your relationship.

Adequate Sleep

Regular adequate sleep is tremendously important to your emotional and physical health. Millions of us suffer from sleep disorders and sleep deprivation. We are a "sleep sick" society.

You have psychobiological rhythms that are as unique to you as your fingerprints. These rhythms affect your sleep, rest, alertness, and performance. One is the circadian rhythm, that 24-hour period of alternation between your sleep and awake times, which is the familiar pattern of approximately sixteen hours awake and eight hours asleep. This varies from individual to individual.

Some research suggests that the single most important factor in predicting longevity is healthful sleep—more than exercise, diet, or heritability.

Another is the ultradian rhythm, which refers to those more than once-a-day cycles of energy, performance, memory, and reaction time. These are periods throughout your day of peak performance lasting approximately 1.5 to 2 hours alternating with rest periods of approximately 15 to 20 minutes—thus, your need for midmorning, midafternoon, and lunch breaks. It is important that you recognize your own rhythms.

What is most relevant for our purpose here is that you become self-aware regarding your rest and sleep needs. No martyrs allowed! Get what you need. It is also important to be informed about the dangers of being deprived of rest and sleep—both to yourself and to your relationship. Being tired can affect everything in your daily life from concentration to coordination to mood regulation. It also has a major impact on your immune system, as well as being linked to heart disease, diabetes, obesity, and mental disorders.

Ideally, it is best if you experience all of the stages of sleep every night. If you have a sleep disorder, this process is interrupted on a somewhat regular basis. As an adult, it is ideal if you spend one third of your life sleeping. You may claim that you can "get by" on four or five hours, but this can eventually lead to problems in your everyday performance and health. Sleep or lack thereof is a huge issue in many relationships.

Sleep experts recommend that adults get eight contiguous hours of sleep each night. Nearly 75% of Americans fail to do so and nearly forty million Americans suffer from one or more of the many varieties of sleep disorders.

The following questions may help you evaluate whether you are getting adequate sleep:

○ **Are you alert?**

○ **Is your energy level adequate?**

○ **Is your health good?**

○ **Is your perception clear?**

○ **Does your memory seem to be accurate?**

○ **Is your reaction time adequate for your safety?**

○ **Are you productive throughout the day?**

○ **Does your creativity seem to be adequate?**

○ **Are you able to communicate effectively?**

○ **Are your moods stable?**

If you answered yes to more than seven of these questions, it is likely that you are not sleep deprived. It is wise to keep this list in mind for those difficult or stressful times when you may not be getting adequate sleep. Sleep deprivation or a sleep disorder can range from annoying to life threatening.

A key question to ask yourself is "Am I really refreshed and feeling rested when I awaken in the morning?"

What does all of this have to do with our relationships and EQ? Sleep is an important ingredient in the mind–body–spirit triad, and it interacts with the other issues discussed in this chapter: diet, exercise, and weight management. There can be powerful effects of sleep or lack thereof on both your mental and physical health.

If you suffer from a lack of sleep and have any of the physical or mental symptoms listed above, you may have difficulty managing your emotions, maintaining a positive attitude, being attuned to your partner, or handling frustrations appropriately—which are all important components of EQ and can strongly affect your marriage.

There are significant improvements in your interactions when one or both of you recover from a sleep disorder or begin to get increased sleep after a period of sleep deprivation.

Although it can be extremely helpful for connecting with and understanding your subconscious processes and your spiritual self, I have chosen not to devote time to the dreaming process or dream analysis because I cannot do justice to this issue within the constraints of this book. Spirituality, the third component of the mind–body–spirit triad, is discussed in detail in Chapter 7.

Proper Nutrition

"Dieting" is not an appropriate way to manage your weight. This is best achieved by long-term lifestyle change not by dieting.

There is a lot of information available to us regarding the interaction be-

How you think and feel is directly affected by what you take into your body.

tween your mind and body in the area of nutrition. There is some truth to the saying, "You are what you eat." Certain foods are "crazy making," and you can suffer emotionally because of what you do or do not eat. Other foods have the opposite effect. For example, a regular intake of B vitamins such as B1, B2, B6, and folic acid in combination with vitamin D and selenium can reduce depression and anxiety significantly in some people. Omega 3 oils and antioxidants found in certain fish may also be helpful for prevention of depression and anxiety, as well as some health problems.

You can get these nutrients through foods such as dairy products, eggs, sardines, lean meat, whole grains, and certain nuts. Or you may prefer taking supplements. Either way, they can boost certain neurotransmitters or chemicals in your brain such as serotonin. This is associated with your mood and appetite regulation, your ability to sleep, and other important functions.

On the other hand, white rice, white potatoes, white bread products (including pastas and tortillas), and products made with white sugar can lead to mood instability because they are relatively empty calories and they are digested quickly and can cause spiking in your blood sugar and a release of insulin. These refined and simple carbohydrates usually stimulate your appetite and can cause you to overeat which, of course, can lead to any number of other problems.

Whole grains, whole wheat, and natural grain breads or bread products are less processed, take longer to digest, do not cause a spike in blood sugar, and provide a much longer feeling of satiety.

If you manage it wisely, a food plan that includes certain fruits such as fresh blueberries, raspberries and strawberries; green vegetables; beans or legumes; proteins; and whole grains is likely to give you both physical and mental benefits. Many of these foods contain antioxidants, which fight free radicals, the molecules that damage cells. And you cannot underestimate the importance of protecting and strengthening your cells, the building blocks of your body. For example, you are not feeding your children important nutrients if you are giving them macaroni and cheese without fresh fruits and vegetables.

Equally controversial is the issue of whether certain herbs and supplements provide health benefits. A popular example is the use of ginkgo biloba, known to boost mental awareness, slow cognitive decline, improve concentration and memory, and enhance abstract reasoning in certain people. Another is the use of calcium, glucosamine, and chondroitin for the strength and health of bones, cartilage, and muscles.

You cannot get all that your body and mind need from the foods you eat. By the time they arrive on your table, many of the nutrients have dissipated or been processed out.[24] Using supplements may be helpful to you as long as you

There is an ongoing debate between the health and fitness industries and the medical community regarding the safety and effectiveness of nutritional supplements.

are well informed or under the care or guidance of someone who has expertise in their effect and safety.

Millions of people in the United States suffer from depression, and you or your partner may be among them. You should consider all available resources to relieve this suffering. The safe use of supplements may be such a resource.

The following example demonstrates the interconnection between diet and mental functioning:

Imbalance in your body chemicals can cause emotional problems, and appropriate dietary changes can restore your brain's equilibrium.

There is no question that our diet/nutritional intake can have a significant effect on our mental or emotional functioning. One interesting case of this phenomenon was that of a young man in his late twenties who had suffered years of depression. Mark had been suicidal, socially isolated, and academically and professionally underfunctioning. He had a very poor diet, rarely eating anything of nutritional value. He came to me while in the midst of a divorce and after having undergone previous psychotherapy and ingesting numerous psychotropics. After several months of treatment Mark began to report that as a result of our work together and an improved diet (which I encouraged), he was beginning to feel better about himself and his life.

Mark remarried and began to improve in all areas of functioning, and I soon learned that his new wife was an excellent cook who insisted that he eat a nutritious diet on a regular basis. He eventually terminated therapy, reduced his psychotropic intake, returned to school, started a new job, and bought a starter home with his wife. I am not naive enough to believe that a simple change in diet is a panacea for depression. In this case, the impact of appropriate psychotherapy, a meaningful relationship with a love partner, and a change in body chemistry due to improved nutrition all contributed significantly to an improved quality of life for this young man. Mark's experience is only one of many I have witnessed in which a change in diet had a noticeable positive impact on emotional stability and mental functioning.

Consistent Exercise

Your body is designed to be moving not to be sitting. It might seem that the amount of information available to us on the physical benefits of exercise borders on "overkill." But we need this information. Less than half the U.S. population participates in a regular exercise regimen. And exercise does stimulate your immune system, which results in less illness, generally makes you stronger, reduces your stress, and rejuvenates you.

There are numerous mental health benefits of being physically active. For example, regular exercise is advantageous for mood regulation (a component of EQ) and is known to combat depression and anxiety. In some cases it can be more effective than psychotropic medications; in others it will enhance their effects.

If you exercise regularly, you are also likely to have better self-esteem and a sense of overall well-being. It may even boost your ability to think more clearly or at a higher level. Can you see that each of these benefits has the potential to improve your interactions with others and ideally create healthier love relationships?

Clearly, exercise heightens positive feelings and thoughts and reduces negative ones. It is well known that certain peptides or chemicals such as endorphins, enkephalins, and adrenaline are released in most of us when we exercise, and tend to enhance our mood. Some studies show that the interruption of a regular fitness regimen can even cause mood disturbances.

Try to choose a consistent regular exercise program that is as much a part of your life as going to work, sleeping, or preparing a meal. It will be less effective or you will abandon it if you don't make it a regular part of your life. This requires self-motivation, persistence, and the managing of emotions to maintain a consistent regimen.

Your choice of an exercise regimen should be based on something you consider to be enjoyable or fun.

It is best to add exercise to your schedule as a lifetime commitment not as a temporary activity. If your fitness program is drudgery, boring, or challenging beyond your limits, you may not stick with it. As you may have experienced, there are inevitable setbacks in a fitness regimen. The EQ ability to maintain enthusiasm and persistence in the face of these setbacks is so important. This is the time to keep going! You and your partner can help each other to be persistent and disciplined.

While our primary concern here is with the emotional and mental health benefits of exercise, let's look at the obvious physical benefits as well. These are numerous, with the most common being lowering your blood pressure, increasing your good cholesterol (high-density lipoprotein), strengthening your heart, increasing your endurance, strengthening your muscles, and enhancing your immune system.

Weight training or exercises designed for muscle strengthening are becoming more popular with both men and women of all ages. One of the most significant benefits is improving your muscle-to-fat ratio, which raises your metabolism and causes your body to burn fuel faster, even when you are asleep. Weight training also builds up your bone density, which can forestall osteoporosis, a great concern to women as they age.

Here are two brief examples of the personal benefits of consistent exercise:

Jerry was a divorced man in his mid-50s who held a stressful job, had poor eating habits, and had a tendency to drink too much. He had been single for several years and although he was dating somewhat, he lived a life that was much too sedentary. He was beginning to experience depression and came into therapy to address the depression and discuss relationship issues. After several sessions, I convinced Jerry of the value of a more active lifestyle; and he began to engage in a consistent exercise regimen and to cut back on his drinking. Within several weeks his depression had lessened, he reported feeling much better about his life, and was more optimistic about the prospects of finding a life partner.

Another example is another man, also in his mid-50s, who had recently married for the second time. Martin and his new wife were doing reasonably well in their relationship, but he was plagued by self-doubt that was residual from his early life experience with an extremely negative and critical mother. He had made some gains in our previous therapy on the damaging effects of this upbringing but was still not feeling motivated and self-accepting in his semi-retired lifestyle. Martin knew that he felt much better about himself and his life when he rode his outdoor bike on a regular basis, and so his homework in therapy was to commit to a regular riding regimen. Like Jerry in the previous example, Martin reported significant increases in energy, positive attitude, weight loss, and self-esteem as he put this regimen into practice. His improved sense of well-being allowed him to make some significant life decisions regarding his retirement and post-retirement employment.

If you have already experienced improvements in your emotional health, overall well-being, and relationship through regular exercise, these examples may seem "ho hum." But it is an inspiration to see this happen for people as a new experience or a resurrection of something that has been of benefit to them in the past. Exercising regularly with your partner can strengthen your relationship and not just your body!

Weight Management

A common issue that bridges diet and exercise is weight management. Dieting for weight loss is not a good idea. There are literally thousands of diets available that make unrealistic promises for beauty and happiness. Of course, you can lose any number of pounds by following one of these many weight-loss programs, but the vast majority of us gain back the weight. There are also potential dangers to your health through "yo-yo" dieting.

It is best to achieve a desired weight and then maintain it as a long-term, lifelong commitment through a nutritional program and fitness plan. This requires regulating or managing your emotions, maintaining hope and optimism, being persistent, delaying gratification, and resisting impulses.

The only thing that works for proper weight management is an ongoing lifestyle of appropriate nutrition and exercise.

While nearly half the U.S. population is overweight and millions are designated as obese, to starve ourselves, exercise excessively, or binge and purge is not the answer.

Have you found yourself being an "emotional eater" to regulate or boost your mood? This is only a temporary fix similar to many other "feel good" escapes such as overspending or watching too much TV. Eating is a very common response to a bad mood or to feeling blue. Some experts say that your moods stimulate your desire for food more than your metabolic processes. Exercise is a more appropriate mood booster—you would be better off to take a brisk walk than to reach for that chocolate brownie or bag of potato chips.

Weight management may not be as important for good mental health as the three previous building blocks: proper diet, exercise, and adequate sleep.

It requires self-awareness and resisting your impulses to refrain from giving in to your cravings— two important qualities of EQ.

But it does play an important role in your physical and emotional health and represents an age-old struggle that has haunted many otherwise healthy relationships. Women are generally more concerned with their weight than men are and, in general, men express more discontent with their wives' weight gain than vice versa. For both, it is a complex, sensitive, often fragile, and potentially explosive issue.

A healthy lifestyle and commitment to fitness can contribute in a positive way to your interactions with your partner. Some of you may believe that your partner is remiss in self-care, and so you ask him/her to address this issue. Perhaps you have struggled with feeling that you are being superficial, petty, or small-minded to insist that he/she maintain physical fitness or an active lifestyle or that they quit smoking or lose weight. You might be haunted by the message that "if I truly loved my partner, this would not matter." It is important to learn to express your needs in relationships. In many cases this includes expressing the need to find your partner attractive and to know they are fit and healthy.

In many marriages the weight management issue centers around physical and sexual attractiveness; for others, it is a genuine concern for the partner's health.

If you are truly emotionally intelligent and mature, can you claim that the physical appearance of your partner due to overweight and/or lack of fitness is a detriment to your attraction to them and subsequent feelings for them?

The answer is, in some cases, yes. An emotionally intelligent person handles this issue with compassion, empathy, maturity, and attunement, but you do not have to deny your true feelings about it. You have a right to address this concern in your relationship.

The process of aging is also related to this issue. Emotional intelligence requires maturity, which may include being realistic about the process of aging. We all change physically as we age, and it is best if you are able to accept this gracefully. Being attractive to your partner should not be about measuring up to cultural expectations of beauty or good looks but about the expectations within your relationship. Attractiveness has always been in the eye of the beholder, as well it should be.

Many women gain weight as they age, some as a consequence of meno-pause. Men do as well. Having a healthy body image, regardless of weight and fitness, is a component of good mental health. It is best if we can accept our-selves just as we are. However, if you have expectations for your partner to be fit and trim, some serious negotiation may be required. Some people cannot maintain an "ideal" weight no matter how hard they try. Fitness and health should be the priority here.

This is different than a situation in which both of you are quite capable of being trim and fit but simply disregard it as a concern of your partner. No matter how you slice it, this is a tough and uncomfortable issue. It requires persistence and self-motivation on the part of the partner who may be remiss in self-care and empathy and optimism on the part of the complaining partner.

A brief example demonstrates how difficult this weight issue can be:

Barbara and Andy had been married for approximately 10 years and had one child. Their relationship had been strained for some time (for a number of reasons), but the "last straw" for both of them was Barbara's weight. Andy claimed that because of her weight gain, Barbara was no longer at-tractive to him. Barbara claimed that he was insensitive and small-minded about this issue, and she wanted to be loved for whom she was despite her weight. They continue to struggle on with their marriage, but it is clear that emotional intelligence on both parts is the key to saving this marriage.

Clearly there are deeper issues here, but for this couple this persistent and painful problem created a nearly insurmountable barrier to healing their mar-riage. I suspect that this may be a somewhat common problem that is swept under the rug and allowed to erode relationships because it is so difficult to talk about and is so powerfully influenced by the culture.

SUMMARY

There are seven particular qualities of EQ that are essential for effectively deal-ing with the issues presented in this chapter. These include:

- **Being self-motivated—managing your emotions to reach a goal**

- Maintaining enthusiasm and persistence in the face of frustration and having the capacity to tolerate defeat

- Delaying gratification and resisting your impulses

- Maintaining a sense of self-efficacy

- Empathizing and being attuned to others, especially your partner, and dealing with them effectively

- Maintaining hope, positive thinking, and optimism

- Being self-aware and having self-knowledge

Two themes of this chapter are that the maintenance of physical health and fitness contributes to good emotional health and vice versa and that both can ultimately contribute to the functioning of your relationships. Maintaining good physical health includes appropriate diet; exercise; stress reduction; an active, healthy lifestyle; and adequate rest. To do what it takes to achieve optimal health in these areas requires you to be *self-motivated*, to *manage your emotions* to reach your goal, and to have an *optimistic attitude*.

This is no easy task because you are faced with easily accessible, super-sized quantities of food; sedentary entertainment escapes such as TV, net surfing, and video games; and increasing stressors on your life at home and in the workplace. For some of us, the challenge feels too great and we are not able to maintain our *enthusiasm and persistence* when we face setbacks or *tolerate* the inevitable *defeats* in our lives. For others of us, it is a welcome challenge to *manage our emotions* to reach certain health, lifestyle, and fitness goals. We can see how these benefit our relationships.

If you have ever had to change your diet for either weight loss or health reasons, you will attest to the fact that it can require tremendous self-discipline, *impulse control*, and *delayed gratification* to refrain from eating your favorite, though inappropriate, foods or to eat the right quantities. The same EQ qualities obviously apply to exercise and other lifestyle issues as well. We may not want to push ourselves to exercise, maintain an active lifestyle, and do what it takes to reduce stress. But if you can learn to manage your emotions and attitude, although difficult, you reap significant rewards and so does your relationship.

As explained in detail in this chapter, having a sense of *self-efficacy* and a *hopeful, positive attitude* contributes to both your physical and mental health.

This, coupled with an ability to be *empathic and attuned to* your partner as he/she struggles to be healthy, can increase the closeness in your relationship. Understanding the mind–body connection and actualizing it in your life require a huge effort, and having the empathy and understanding of your partner can be of great help.

Finally, being aware of and understanding your own feelings, behaviors, attitudes, and beliefs as they relate to the mind–body process pave the way for an essential honesty in your relationship. As is true of so many other aspects of your relationship, *self-awareness* and *self-knowledge* are necessary requirements for dealing with the huge challenges associated with all that goes into optimal physical and mental health. Many factors related to the mind–body processes are sensitive and must be shared with your partner in a gentle, sensitive way.

•   •   •

Now with the mind–body component in order, let's move on to the very personal but important issue of your spirit. Chapter 7 will show how your EQ is related to the spirit aspect of the mind–body–spirit triad and how it inevitably affects your relationship.

CHAPTER SEVEN

Spirituality

Frosting or Foundation?

Faith is the force of life.

—LEO TOLSTOY

Spirituality in your relationship can be viewed either as part of a firm foundation or as something nonessential. That is clearly for you to decide. You may or may not be a particularly religious or spiritually oriented person. Whether you are or not, read on as the pages to follow are likely to challenge your thinking on this issue and perhaps even be enlightening.

This chapter will take you through several steps that will help you understand the role of spirituality and its interface with emotional intelligence (EQ) in your love relationship. These include: what is meant by spirituality, the relationship between your health and your spirituality, and spiritual maturity and spiritual intelligence. Most couples who use a substantial amount of EQ in their relationship reflect a level of holism which includes not just spirituality but spiritual maturity.

Your spirituality is a highly personal and subjective part of your life, but it would be shortsighted to omit the spiritual dimension from a discussion on committed love relationships. This is a potentially valuable resource for certain qualities such as hope, optimism, compassion, and tolerance—all important aspects of EQ and all needed in fully functioning relationships/marriages.

Try to maintain an open mind and to weave your beliefs and understandings into and around those presented here. It is not particularly appropriate for any of us to function at the extreme poles of any religious debate or the religiosity vs. spirituality continuum. Some forms of religion cause guilt and suffering. But generally reasonable religiosity and spiritual practices correlate with good mental health, physical health, and longevity. My perspective is, once again, that this contributes to your EQ and thus congruous interactions.

WHAT IS SPIRITUALITY?

Religion and spirituality are somewhat different but not mutually exclusive constructs. The concept of "spirituality" is used here primarily instead of "religion" because it has a more inclusive and broad meaning.

I am using the term spirituality to mean that human beings have spirits, most have a belief in God, a Universal Force, or a Higher Power, and many believe this is indwelling as well as transcendent. Most traditional faiths or world religions—Christianity, Hinduism, Buddhism, Judaism, Islam, Taoism, and other major paths—are vehicles for helping us seek truths through religious or spiritual teachings about this transcendent and indwelling force. Faith satisfies our need for the following:

- **A deeper meaning in life**

- **A set of personal values**

- **A context for morality**

- **Religious or spiritual practices**

- **Ethical grounding**

- **A consistent world view**

- **A sense of community or belonging to a church, mosque, synagogue, or temple**

A spiritual quest is different from a religious one. A religious pilgrimage is to a known destination and offers specific answers, but a spiritual journey involves an ongoing effort to discover the meaning and sacredness in life and to maintain a continuing quest for a relationship to God/Universal Force. Religion knows; spirituality continues to seek.

In *Hymns to an Unknown God*, Sam Keen, Ph.D., well-known author and theologian, shares, "Because I had been raised by gentle and kindly Christians, I had never seen clearly the hidden cruelty implicit in dogmatic religion . . . (I learned later of) the unloving logic of

Religious thought often claims to have answers, whereas the spiritual quest asks questions and continues to wrestle with the mysteries of God/Universal Force and of life.

fundamentalism that allows true believers to love and respect only those who believe in their version of the truth. Moses, Jesus, Buddha, Confucius, Mohammed, and Lao Tzu make claims about God. But if we concentrate on the experience of the holy, we find there is near-universal agreement."[25]

Most Americans report they feel a need to experience spiritual growth. Even the most scientific among us—physicists, biochemists, astronomers—

However defined or conceptualized, most of us are in search of meaning in life and many for meaning of a spiritual nature.

claim that their quests closely approach the sacred; and many of these individuals think we need to believe in God to experience the sacred.

HOW IS SPIRITUALITY RELATED TO YOUR HEALTH?

This section may seem unrelated to EQ in your relationship. But as Figures 6-1 and 6-2 illustrate, your body, mind, and spirit all interact. And the better you function in each part of yourself, the more likely you are to be emotionally intelligent and to have a better relationship.

First a bit of history: Psychology and medicine have traditionally denied the value of religion and spirituality to mental health and physical healing. Fortunately, this is changing. Studies on the role of spirituality now appear consistently in professional journals in these fields.

Carl Jung was one of the few early major psychologists to connect the spiritual or religious dimension with mental health. His work was groundbreaking and considered outrageous by his contemporaries (1920 to 1960). He believed that religion constituted the meaning of life and played a major role in our psychological processes. He also taught that religious maturity includes a deep respect for other individuals, which we now can see requires EQ.

Jung considered religion or a spiritual journey to be so essential that neglect of your religious needs was seen as a primary cause of neurosis. He claimed that you are healthy emotionally only if you gain or regain a religious attitude. He said that he didn't just believe God existed, he knew he existed.

In contrast, Sigmund Freud saw religion as corrosive to human happiness; it created obsessions and other neuroses and led to repressed sexuality, guilt, and the suppression of feelings. Most of the early major schools of thought in psychology saw religion and spirituality as mental instability.

Currently, among medical doctors and mental health professionals, there is an increasing respect for the role of spirituality and religiosity.

The spiritual dimension of life is being recognized in medicine and psychology as too important to be ignored.

Sometimes religion can have a negative influence on your life and your relationships. For example, there is potential danger in believing in an angry and punishing God. A healthy view of religion and spirituality and a respect for diversity of religious perspectives requires EQ and adds a measure of dimension to your life, including your relationships.

The term "psychospiritual" represents the blending of these two important dimensions of your life. The religious or spiritual dimension can bring something special to your life and help with some of your basic problems. Some of the questions you wrestle with cannot be viewed from a purely psychological perspective. Your struggles may have a deeply profound existential, spiritual meaning. This may even include your effort to create and sustain a healthy love relationship.

A spiritual practice can help us control and modulate our strong and negative emotions. This is the foundation for EQ.

For example, meditation or deep contemplative prayer can help with all aspects of your life, including the control or management of your emotions.

Meditation and/or prayer can:

- Help you consciously control your behaviors

- Increase your self-awareness and help you expose the blind spots about yourself

- Help you learn techniques for dealing with depression and panic states or anxiety

- Relieve your illnesses by lowering distress and anxiety and reducing pain and muscle tension

- Lower your blood pressure, oxygen consumption, and heart rate

- Help you control your negative thoughts and feelings

Use the above as a checklist to determine if any of these items are useful to you. The January 2003 *American Psychologist* reports current research pointing toward a link between health and wellness and religions or spiritual practices. You have the seeds of happiness and health within you, and these habits can help you connect with this and pave the way for greater EQ.

Doctors are combining patients' religious or spiritual beliefs with state of the art medical treatments because of the evidence that points to the positive effects of religion and spirituality on our health. They are observing strong connections between religious beliefs and life satisfaction, hope, and purpose—

all of which help us heal. Some doctors will even take your spiritual history as well as your medical history, an idea that was considered outrageous until recently.

If you believe that you will be punished by God for wrongdoing, this can pose a problem when you are faced with illness. Medical professionals should avoid manipulating you or imposing their beliefs if they are contradictory to your belief that faith can bring healing.

When a psychospiritual approach is used, treatment is tailored to suit your preferences or beliefs. If you are Catholic, you might choose to recite the rosary; if Buddhist or Hindu, to repeat a chant or to meditate; if nonreligious, to use affirmations or repetitious phrases; or if you are Protestant Christian, you might choose to pray or quote scripture. Whatever the case, diversity must be expected and honored and your individual choices respected.

SPIRITUAL MATURITY AND SPIRITUAL INTELLIGENCE

Clearly, EQ in general and in relationships requires you to be mature. We have looked at other aspects of emotional maturity; here we will explore spiritual maturity and spiritual intelligence. It is not enough to just be a religious or spiritual person to have a stronger relationship. Your religiosity and spirituality need to be mature and intelligent if you wish to maximize the satisfaction between you and your partner.

Mature spirituality can be important for a truly healthy, functional, and fulfilling marriage.

This is not to suggest a simplistic position that "the couple who prays together stays together." You don't even have to share the same spiritual path, although this may be more fun and interesting. Millions of us attend churches, temples, mosques, or synagogues on a regular basis, but our faith lacks the depth called for here. The more emotionally intelligent you are, the more likely you are to be emotionally and spiritually mature and vice versa.

In the words of Marsha Sinetar, educator, corporate advisor, and author, "Spirituality is not just an abstract, blissed-out or purposeless emotion, nor an out-of-reach, mythical goal. Spirituality is an intelligence in its own right: useful, tactical, and immensely creative. With a high spiritual IQ we gain insight, wisdom, visionary or strategic, big-picture perceptual skills and the knack of right action . . . This has everything to do with our growing in personal power and tangible, lasting, real world effectiveness and little to do with that dreamy, aimless quality so often equated with spirituality . . . To increase spiritual intelligence . . . we first give of ourselves . . . improve our self-discipline and our responsibility-taking skills."[26] EQ!

Unfortunately many of us do not develop maturity in our religious or spiritual beliefs. This has been proven to have a detrimental effect on other aspects of life, including love relationships.

Throughout the centuries writers, theologians, religious leaders, and great thinkers have contributed a wealth of information and wisdom on religion and spirituality. If you are interested in the views of such individuals, please consult Appendix C. It provides a brief outline of six renowned contributors who gave us a framework for spiritual maturity and its relationship to EQ.

SPIRITUALITY IN LOVE RELATIONSHIPS

Without question, mature spirituality refines and
purifies our interpersonal lives.

—MARSHA SINETAR

Ideally spiritual growth leads to changes and improvements in your personal habits, behaviors, and interactions, including those most intense with a committed partner. The role of spirituality in your committed love relationship is twofold. First, the more spiritually evolved/mature you are, the more likely it is that you will also be emotionally mature. Secondly, spiritual maturity increases your chances of being hopeful, tolerant, and empathic, which are key characteristics of EQ. If you are a person of faith, you are generally mentally healthier, and again, one of the basic premises in this book is that mentally healthy people create healthier relationships. Church attendance or even active involvement in a religious institution does not by itself lead to spiritual maturity. Millions of us show up at a church, mosque, synagogue, or temple every week and actively follow religious paths that tend to be stifling to us and do not promote acceptance of others' beliefs or needs.

If you are a happy person, you are more likely to have the characteristics listed below. They are encouraged in most faiths and reflect EQ as well. You may want to use this as a checklist and ask yourself if your faith makes you a happier, healthier person and if you exhibit these qualities:

- Less self-focused
- Less judgmental
- Less critical of others
- Less self-righteous
- Energetic
- Decisive
- Less hostile and abusive
- More trusting
- Sociable
- More loving and forgiving
- Helpful
- Creative
- More hopeful and positive

This is not to say that nonreligious or nonspiritual people are unhappy. But if you are happier, you are more appealing as a partner because you are more likely to be good-natured, outgoing, and appropriately focused on others.

As in other areas of maturity and EQ, it is ideal if you and your partner can be "on the same page" spiritually. But that is not always necessary. What is most important is that you are both spiritually mature and that you both maintain a respect and tolerance for each other's beliefs and practices. If you are at different levels in your spiritual or religious development, with one of you being more mature or evolved than the other, this can create difficulty for you as a couple.

In other words, having differences in your specific belief systems or religious affiliations is not the problem! The problem is the difference in your level of spiritual development or maturity.

A brief but touching example illustrates this situation:

Martha and Jack had been married for nearly thirty years. She chose many years ago not to be a "believer" or participate in any religious practice or organization due to a very hurtful experience with a pastor in her teen years. Her husband was a lifelong Catholic. They each respected the other's chosen path. They did not bother to debate religion, which is always a wise choice. Motivated in part by her struggle with anxiety, Martha recently began opening up to the idea of God as a Universal Power who exists beyond her earthly limitations—this idea made her feel safe and gave her hope. While this has not had a huge impact on their marriage, Martha reports some enhancement of intimacy and attunement with Jack because they are now able to resonate to some degree on a spiritual level. He had felt inadequate in his ability to help her with her anxiety, and so they both are experiencing her spiritual growth as a helpful resource. And all of this was possible without spending thirty years battling over their religious differences or trying to convince the other to believe as they do!

In general, if you are more mature spiritually, you will bring more courage, joy, openness, compassion, and understanding to your marriage or committed relationship—all are aspects of EQ. Unlike the other relationship issues addressed in previous chapters such as healing of your past (Chapter 2), expressing intimacy (Chapter 3), listening and managing conflict (Chapter 4), developing your self-esteem (Chapter 5), and the like, the topic of spirituality involves more than prescribed skills or actions. Instead, it involves your specific character traits and to some degree your personality style. There is clearly an interface between this and all other aspects of relationships and displays of EQ, but it is unique and idiosyncratic depending upon your individual spiritual path or beliefs.

SUMMARY

Mature spirituality involves a kind of "spiritual intelligence." Additionally, there are five particular EQ qualities that are necessary for healthy spiritual functioning individually and in a committed relationship.

These EQ qualities include:

1. Maintaining a sense of self-efficacy

2. Empathizing and being attuned to others and dealing with them effectively

3. Maintaining hope, positive thinking, and an attitude of optimism

4. Being self-aware and having self-knowledge

5. Maintaining persistence in the face of frustration and tolerating defeat

If mature spirituality involves an open mind, taking responsibility, absence of a fear of God as the "scary judge in the sky," and a genuine search for truth, then you must have a relatively strong sense of self-efficacy to achieve this in as many areas of your life as possible. You will feel powerless and like a victim or mere pawn if you depend completely upon some external power as a puppeteer controlling all aspects of your life; or, if you view what happens to you in life as a mere "crap shoot" based only on some horrible fate. With an *efficacious attitude*, we believe in our ability to deal with life's challenges and that we can have some influence over certain outcomes. Having a very strong faith in God does not mean you cannot believe in your own abilities and personal power. The theological concept of cocreation applies here. This means that we are working in conjunction with God in influencing the outcomes of our lives and in many cases the lives of others. This is a huge responsibility not to be taken lightly.

As with nearly all other aspects of a committed love relationship, *empathy* and *attunement* are essential for both your individual spiritual journey and that shared with your partner. This is particularly true if one or both of you is experiencing a period of doubt or some other struggle with your religious or spiritual beliefs. It can also be necessary to be very *attuned* to your partner and *empathetic* if the two of you have significant differences in your beliefs and practices.

A person of faith, particularly one who has a mature or intelligent faith, is grounded in an enduring sense of *hope, optimism, and positive thinking*. Notwithstanding serious emotional problems such as depression and the inevitable difficult times when we experience great pain and hopelessness, this component of EQ is a mark of a truly spiritual person. Perhaps we have all encountered angry, judgmental, frightened individuals who claim they are very religious. Seems oxymoronic, doesn't it?

It can be quite effective in your relationship when one of you can maintain the *hope and optimism* and see life's glass as half full if the other loses his/her spiritual or emotional footing. What could be more reassuring and loving?

And finally, as is true in all areas of a relationship, to be spiritually mature requires *self-awareness and self-knowledge*. We all use denial at times or tend to believe things about ourselves that are not true. Or we refuse to face up to things that are true but difficult to accept. In the realm of religiousness or spirituality, this can be particularly troublesome because it often leads to being judgmental and self-righteous. For good mental health and the health of your relationship, understand yourself and be as self-honest as possible regarding your religious or spiritual path and process. Humility and self-disclosure pay big dividends here.

●   ●   ●

In Part III, we move on to the "how to's": specific guidelines and exercises for developing your EQ to a level that can help to enhance your interactions with your love partner. You no doubt want to improve yourself and your relationship, so dive in and take the challenge.

PART III

CHAPTER EIGHT

How to Increase Emotional Intelligence for Your Relationship

Emotional intelligence is a way of recognizing,
understanding, and choosing how we think, feel,
and act. It shapes our interactions with
others and our understanding of ourselves.

—JOSHUA M. FREEDMAN, ANABEL L. JENSEN, MARSHA C.
RIDEOUT, & PATRICIA E. FREEDMAN IN *HANDLE WITH CARE:
EMOTIONAL INTELLIGENCE ACTIVITY BOOK*

Part III (Chapters 8 to 15) provides you with guidelines and recommendations on how you might further develop your emotional intelligence (EQ). It is best if you think of this process as building on your strengths and on what is "right with you" instead of thinking you are starting from scratch and that there is something "wrong with you." We all have some degree of EQ.

Use Part III as a workbook. Each chapter contains very specific guidelines and suggestions to help you develop a specific aspect of EQ. Just reading through the book thus far and completing the exercises and self-tests in various chapters should have contributed to your EQ to some degree. What you will find in Chapters 8 to 15 will get you well on your way to developing the EQ you need to improve your relationship.

You can learn a great deal by hearing a lecture or reading a book, which are left brain functions. But an even more powerful and lasting way to learn for many of us is experiential or doing something that involves action on our part—something that is "hands on." You will find both experiential and cognitive learning opportunities offered here.

The nine characteristics of EQ as applied in all seven chapters thus far include:

1. Having self-awareness and self-knowledge

2. Knowing, understanding, regulating or managing your emotions, and expressing or using them appropriately and adaptively

3. Empathizing and being attuned to others, especially your partner, and dealing with them effectively

4. Maintaining hope, positive thinking, and an attitude of optimism

5. Keeping distress from swamping your ability to think—being able to override negative emotions or moods to be able to think and function appropriately

6. Maintaining enthusiasm and persistence in the face of frustration or setbacks and having the capacity to tolerate defeat

7. Maintaining a sense of self-efficacy

8. Delaying gratification and controlling or resisting your impulses, both emotionally and in actions

9. Being self-motivated—managing your emotions to reach a goal

This book is for everyone. If you are someone who is interested in personal growth and in improving your relationship and making it more satisfying, this process is for you. If you are content with things just as they are or are faint hearted when it comes to hard work, you might still be inspired. Developing your EQ is rewarding, but it can require a lot of work depending upon your starting point.

The terms "qualities," "skills," "abilities," "components," "characteristics," and "aspects" are all used interchangeably as we discuss the development of EQ.

In an extensive review of the literature, I identified some 350 books and articles on EQ. Most writers do not address the issue of how to develop or increase your EQ, and those who do are focused primarily on career/workplace or school/education environments. In the business world, EQ is directed toward being stable, self-controlled, hardworking, goal oriented, and understanding others so that you can influence them. The chapters in this section bring more heart into the use of EQ because the focus is on love relationships.

To be sure, some of the EQ qualities encouraged in work/school settings are also applicable to personal relationships: self-motivation, persistence, delaying gratification, positive thinking, impulse control, and self-control. However, these must be applied in a relationship/marriage with self-awareness, love, great empathy and compassion, and a desire to be attuned to a loved one for understanding, not just for achieving goals or influencing each other. Here, EQ is used for altruistic purposes and is centered in deep caring for the enhancement of the relationship.

CAN YOU CHANGE?

Can you change? Can you develop or increase your EQ? Does this involve changes in your personality? Is your personality created by "nature" or "nurture?" Yes. Qualified yes . . . Somewhat . . . And both . . . Obviously various mental health fields claim that we can change, heal, grow, and at a minimum, stabilize. That is what we are committed to. Have you heard people protest, "I can't change my entire personality" or "I can't change who I am" or "I am who I am"? While becoming more emotionally intelligent requires you to make some changes, it is not a matter of transforming your basic personality. It involves either resurrecting your hidden qualities or adding on to and enhancing who and what you are.

WHAT IS PERSONALITY?

There are numerous definitions of personality. One very basic, workable definition is that it is consistent behavior patterns and intrapersonal processes originating from within. These patterns and processes are referred to as "individual differences." They include behaviors, emotions, motivations, and thoughts. Personality is formed by genetic heritage, physiology, early life experience, and ongoing developmental process. It is mostly set in the early years but sometimes changes dramatically throughout your life span.

There are divergent theories of how personality is formed, all of which make a valuable contribution to our understanding of ourselves. Most common among them are psychoanalytical, trait, biological/physiological, humanistic, behavioral/social learning, cognitive, neo-Freudian, and systems theory. Each of these is defined in Appendix A.

While EQ concerns mostly the way you use and manage your feelings or emotions and those of others, it also influences the other aspects of your personality as well—your behaviors, motivations, and thinking processes. And all of these can be developed or improved! In a 1998 article in the *Harvard Business Review* entitled "Can Emotional Intelligence be Learned?", Goleman provides a word of encouragement. He says that EQ can be inborn or genetically influenced as well as socially determined or learned. It increases in some of us with age and maturity but can be learned or further developed in people of all ages if the right part of the brain, the limbic system, is targeted in this effort.

Goleman is primarily addressing EQ as it applies to the work setting, but this applies to personal relationships as well.

Your entire brain plays a role in emotion, but it is the brain's limbic system that is most important in processing emotions and associated activities. It is responsible primarily for emotional behavior and reactivity, impulses, drives, certain motivations, and the storage of memories. The parts of the brain included in this system are called the amygdala, hippocampus, and hypothalamus. The limbic system is a key area that needs to be activated, utilized, further developed, or healed if you are interested in increasing your EQ.

To begin, you will need at least a minimal level of certain EQ qualities such as self-awareness, self-motivation, and enthusiasm to further develop others. How quickly you develop the necessary EQ aptitudes required for a smoothly running relationship/marriage depends to some degree on whether you already have the seeds of them in your personal repertoire.

Improving EQ is helpful to anyone, even those with serious mood disorders or other mental or emotional illnesses. However, some individuals will have a great deal of difficulty managing their emotions and behaviors and may have to rely to some degree on professional help.

An important reminder as you proceed—your genetic and physiological make-up can play a significant role in the development of EQ. This can be an asset or a stumbling block for you, but almost anything is possible with effort. Another important thing to keep in mind is that you cannot change your intelligence quotient (IQ) much at all. You can become more knowledgeable and more educated, but your basic functioning IQ is relatively fixed. However, most of us have great potential for developing or growing emotionally—for increasing EQ. It can be a lifetime process of becoming aware of and using your feelings.

Stop and think about a stubborn habit you have broken or a difficult skill you have had to develop. Before you achieved any significant growth, learned this skill, or found a way to break a habit and establish a new one, you had to be seriously committed to the process and motivated to "do what it takes." The same applies to increasing your EQ. This may not be easy for everyone. As it relates to close relationships, the process requires the things listed below.

Ponder this list to determine whether you are ready to proceed on this journey.

- **Concerted, consistent effort.**

- **Sincere, enthusiastic desire to change.**

- Open mind.

- Willingness to participate in honest self-examination.

- Nondefensive ability to take feedback and appropriate criticism from others.

- Following the suggestions in Chapters 9 to 15.

- Getting outside help.

- "Overlearning" and daily application.

- Practice, practice, practice! Growth does not happen quickly.

Part III of this book does not contain a simplistic list of suggestions of "dos and don'ts" and "how tos." It would be easy to promise that if you just "do this" or "do that" your life will be transformed. Developing EQ is far too complex for that. Many of us cannot make major life changes until we overcome certain psychological obstacles or let go of deep-seated habits, patterns, beliefs, and attitudes.

You will be directed to both external and internal resources which, if utilized fully, can have a significant impact. These resources will reinforce already ongoing efforts for some of you and provide a beginning for others. The development or enhancement of certain components of EQ may require professional help or even psychotherapy. Other EQ qualities may be improved through various forms of self-help and personal effort. For some of you, it may take years; for others, only a few months. Either way, it is worth the journey.

For those of you who develop EQ with ease, there is much less need to "bite the bullet" or agonize when things come up in life and in relationships which require these abilities. But for those who are significantly lacking these skills, this deficit can be emotionally painful and lead to trouble or dysfunction in your love relationship. While we want to approach this process with optimism, one warning is in order. If extremely lacking in EQ, you are likely to be unable to use your inherent gifts or full potential; to collapse and be unable to function properly when things get really tough in your close personal relationships; and to find yourself in trouble due to insensitivity, intolerance, impatience, impulsivity, hopelessness, or acting out.

In other words, living and relating without EQ really does have a down side. So why not take the challenge?

The techniques outlined in Part III are applicable to the nine EQ aspects, all of which overlap. For example, the "managing of emotions" and "effective use of emotions" are fundamental themes that are a key part of several other components. Likewise, self-efficacy clearly relates to self-confidence, which is required for persistence. In short, many of the EQ components feed into, enhance, or undergird others; as you develop one, another may fall into place.

As you ponder each of these, remember an important point made earlier— they all require maturity.

While one of your goals is likely to be that of having healthy relationships, you are, first and foremost, a separate individual. The qualities of EQ are valuable to you as an individual as well as to your relationships.

Healthy marriages or relationships are created by adults, not overgrown children in grown-up bodies!

SO HOW DO I DO THIS?

Ultimately, it is a healthy and whole individual coupled with another healthy and whole individual that creates a good relationship.

CHAPTER NINE

Begin with Self-Awareness

Everything that irritates us about others can lead us
to an understanding of ourselves.

—CARL JUNG, M.D.

Know thyself.

—SOCRATES

I t is easy to just pass through life in a somewhat unconscious state and never stop to examine yourself, *why* you are, or *who* you are. There is nothing particularly wrong with that until you decide you want or need to learn something new that may require you to change. It is likely that, if you want your relationship to be more satisfying or run more smoothly, you are going to have to understand yourself and your partner better.

This component is addressed first because it provides the foundation for all aspects of your emotional intelligence (EQ). Without self-awareness and self-understanding, you cannot fully develop any of the other qualities. Also, many of the techniques for improving your self-awareness can be used for other aspects of EQ. This will become clear as you proceed.

First, we look at why it is so important to be self-aware and to understand yourself. Next, a lengthy section guides you in what to look for and to ask when doing self-examination. Finally, the following specific techniques are provided for you: self-observation; reading/bibliotherapy; observing others; participating in workshops, classes, and seminars; and taking personality tests or profiles. If you find only one or two things in this chapter that resonate with you or that are helpful to you, consider it a step forward! That is success!

Use each of the checklists, self-inventories, and exercises as tools to help you get to know yourself better.

If you want to do your part in creating a good relationship, you have to know what you are feeling, what your motives and intentions are, what you need and desire, how you are perceived by others, and generally how you conduct yourself. The concepts of "living consciously" and "mindfulness" convey essentially the same meaning. We're talking here about being introspective because a healthy dose of introspection can make you a good partner.

Keep in mind, as you proceed, that it is best to focus on how all this shows up currently. In other words, focus on beginning right here, right now! For example, you are more likely to stop drinking if you see that you may be drinking too much or drinking in a destructive way right now. The same applies to such things as overeating, how you apply yourself at work, how you come across to others, and how well you know and express your emotions. And if change is not called for, just being your best or "at the top of your game" requires this awareness or self-understanding.

There are differences between *knowing* yourself and *understanding* yourself. Self-awareness tells you how you behave, what you feel and believe, how you come across to others, what your strengths and weaknesses are, etc. Self-knowledge helps to explain how you got to be this way and why it is so. If you see yourself realistically and accurately, it will help you better understand your partner or spouse.

PUT YOURSELF UNDER THE MICROSCOPE

Before you read the next few pages, keep in mind that you have the ability to change the influence of your history and early life experiences. In other words, it is the "nurture" part of the "nature vs. nurture" debate that you are most often able to heal from, change the results of, or build upon.

Some experts claim that your past is not really that important in the formation of your personality. I happen to disagree with this opinion.

For most people, examining your past or personal history helps you to know and understand yourself better. Failing to go through this process is like erecting a building without a foundation. Try to look at how you functioned or behaved as a child and at those people and experiences or influences that affected your development and your view of close relationships and intimacy.

Think about the messages, relationships, and behaviors of key figures in your early years that may have contributed to your level of or lack of the nine qualities of EQ. One important example is that children raised with empathy are more likely to treat others with empathy.

Avoid "overpathologizing"—focusing only on how "sick" you are or on what is wrong with you. Acknowledge your strengths and what is right with you, but at the same time don't gloss over or deny wounds and painful unfinished business. Balance is the key—recognize and build upon the positive influences which helped to make you who you are, but don't overlook any negative influences or unfinished business that may haunt you.

Some of the checklists and self-inventories that follow appear redundant. Remember, your EQ skills overlap. Ponder these lists carefully.

The questions below will help you get started on the path to understanding yourself. A reminder: each of these has to do with some component of EQ.

The term "others" refers primarily to your parents and other family members. There are probably thousands of questions you could ask yourself, but these are specifically related to EQ.

As a child:

- Do you recall knowing that the needs and desires of others were as important as yours? Or did you regularly insist on having your own way and pout if your desires were thwarted? How do you handle this now?

- Did you learn early on to be a good sport? Or were you devastated if you lost while playing a game? What about now?

- Were you willing to complete homework or household chores? Or did you resist being given responsibility? And now?

- Did you persist and try to achieve goals? Or did you give up easily and claim you "couldn't" complete things? How are you at persisting now?

- Did you know that some degree of failure was just a part of life? Or if you failed at something (academic or otherwise), did you either declare yourself hopeless or blame someone else? How about now?

- Did you learn quickly that life doesn't always go your way? Or did you have a difficult time being told "no" when you wanted something? How about now?

- Could you let certain things just "roll off"? Or were you hurt easily? And now?

- Were you sensitive to the feelings of others? Or did you often hurt others? How sensitive to others' feelings are you now?

- Were you able to take some of the tough times in stride? Or did you overreact emotionally and find it hard to handle stress or other difficulties? How do you handle stressful situations now?

- ○ Did you face things head on and have a sense of power over your life? Or did you feel you could not make things better through your own efforts and often feel like a victim of circumstance? How much personal power over your life do you feel now?

- ○ Were you expected to be kind and sensitive to others? Or were kindness and sensitivity to others not taught to you? Are you able to be kind and sensitive to others now?

- ○ Were you taught to be attuned to the feelings of others and to empathize with them? Can you do this now?

- ○ Did anyone teach you to listen attentively? Or were listening and tuning in not treated as important skills in early years? Do you tune in and listen well now?

- ○ Did you feel as though you were seen, noticed, and attended to? Or did you feel invisible to those around you? Do you feel visible now?

- ○ Were you heard and listened to? Or did you feel that your voice was stifled and your words ignored? Do you feel heard by others now?

- ○ Did anyone tune in to you and make you feel as though you were very important to them? Or did you feel as though no one was aware of who you really were or what you were capable of? Do you feel important to others now?

Of course, most of us act out as small children and as teens. The real problem is not outgrowing these negative or immature habits. Sometimes this comes from being overindulged. If you were catered to and allowed to believe you were the "center of the universe" or you were given too much and life was made too easy, you may be intolerant of others. You may also think of yourself as superior to others and lack genuine empathy for those who have had more difficult lives. This can also lead to difficulty with delaying gratification or facing up to the serious challenges that you may face now.

Conversely, this same pattern can come from having your needs neglected or being raised by harsh, demanding parents. For many of us, certain attitudes, behaviors, and feelings don't "show up" until our adult years but are rooted in early influences. Below are some common parenting styles or other situations that may have lead to your current level of EQ.

Did the adult(s) who raised you:

- Teach you how to tune in to others and use empathy and compassion?

- Insist that you manage the way in which you expressed your emotions or related to others?

- Lead you to believe you were equal to others? Inferior? Superior?

- Hold you accountable? Do too much for you?

- Believe it was loving and appropriate to make your decisions for you?

- Teach you to be autonomous? Fight your battles for you?

- Require you to do your homework? Or complete it for you?

- Require that you do household chores? Or cater to you?

- Require you to be involved in character-building extracurricular activities?

- Hold you accountable for your own mistakes?

- Require you to wait for the things and experiences you desired?

- Show compassion for you when you were hurting or troubled?

- Listen to you when you needed to talk?

- Teach you that life can be really tough sometimes, but that difficulties can be handled gracefully?

- Teach you to modulate your emotions or allow emotional overreactivity?

Your parents or caregivers may have been overly controlling or too impatient to teach you how to manage your own behaviors, feelings, and relationships. This parenting approach is often based on such beliefs as "it's easier for me to do things myself than try to get the kids to do it," "it's easier to just give in," "kids will be kids," "I need to protect my children from the difficult things in life that I had to endure," or "we are the (Joneses, Smiths, etc.) and are better than others." If they took the easy route, this may have left you without the EQ resources you now need.

Another common parental style is that of being very critical or harsh. Did you hear any of the following messages—either spoken or implied? Stop and think about whether any of these haunt you today.

- "You never do anything right."

- "You shouldn't feel that way."

- "Children are to be seen and not heard."

- "I am the parent and I always know best."

- "You will never amount to anything."

- "Why can't you be like _____?"

- "Being kind and loving to others is being a wimp!"

- "Do things my way."

- "Who asked you? You are only a child."

- "If you're going to cry, I'll give you something to cry about."

- "How could you be so stupid?"

- "You can do better than that!"

- "I expect you to live up to *my* standards."

- "I make the rules around here!"

If you were punished (as opposed to disciplined) unfairly, you may have decided preconsciously that you may as well not even bother to try. Or you may have developed the habit of being angry, aggressive, or defensive when confronted, challenged, or critiqued. Do you find that you are defensive in the face of challenges or critiques? How do you react to criticism? From friends? Employers? Your partner?

And, of course, if you experienced physical, emotional, or sexual abuse, you may have developed an attitude of hopelessness, helplessness, an inability to trust, and/or discomfort with your feelings and those of others.

Do you think too much was expected of you as a child or adolescent? Were you overwhelmed with responsibilities or expectations beyond your capacity? You could be one of those people who lack the capacity to keep going or to persist because this sense of being overwhelmed was carried over into your adult years. A common example of this is being "parentified" after a divorce or the death of one of your parents. This "role reversal" might have given you the responsibilities once handled by a parent. Also, one or both parents may have had emotional or mental problems and leaned on you for support, which is beyond a child's capacity to handle.

Children sometimes enjoy this power at first, but it eventually becomes an unmanageable burden. This situation can lead in your adult years to feeling easily overwhelmed and defeated or to wielding power inappropriately in your close relationships, including marriage. Take a minute, sit down, and think or journal some of your thoughts and feelings about this. Does it apply to you?

Some people feel that they benefited from having too much expected of them as children. We are all different. The real issue is: How does it affect your close relationships today?

Let's take a look now at how your parents or influential adults may or may not have displayed EQ themselves.

Did your parents or powerful role models:

○ **Allow graciously for others' mistakes? Or demand perfection of other people?**

○ **Listen to others very well? Or fail to listen to people attentively?**

○ **Appear to be very compassionate? Or show little empathy for others?**

○ **Respect the autonomy of other people? Or try to control other people?**

- ○ Display warmth and affection to others? Or withhold nurturing or affection?

- ○ Appear to get discouraged and give up easily? Or display internal motivation or self-discipline?

- ○ Display patience and restraint? Or get easily frustrated and impatient, and "fly off the handle?"

- ○ Use restraint in their actions and words? Or act or speak impulsively?

- ○ Delay their gratification? Or get whatever they wanted as soon as they felt the desire?

- ○ Hold themselves accountable when appropriate? Or blame others for their difficulties?

- ○ Stop to think before they expressed anger or disappointment? Or lash out inappropriately?

- ○ Allow their softer feelings to be displayed? Or convey the message that it was best to be stoic and "tough?"

Give some serious thought to this before you move on. If any of these scenarios are familiar, think about how they may be influencing you now. Perhaps if you jot down some thoughts, feelings, or memories, they will lead you to valuable clues about yourself.

Did your parents or caretakers convey any of the following message (either directly/indirectly or spoken/unspoken)?

- ○ The feelings of others are very important. Or the feelings of others do not matter.

- ○ It can be very rewarding to be close to people. Or being emotionally close is unnecessary or even dangerous.

- ○ Everyone's feelings are important, even yours. Or my feelings matter more than yours.

- ○ Life can be a challenge, but we can handle it. Or life is too difficult.

- ° Everyone is capable. They just need to use their capabilities. Or I am not capable. Let someone else do it.

- ° Never give up. Don't be a victim. Or life is unfair and terrible—there is no hope.

- ° Listen to your heart and emotions as well as your thoughts. Or use your head, not your heart.

- ° Always consider the rights and needs of others as well as your own. Or go after what you want without regard for others.

- ° You and your feelings are just as important as anyone else's. Or others are always more important than you. Your worth or feelings do not matter.

Ask yourself if you believe or live by any of these now. The checklist above will help you identify any EQ skills on which you need to work.

Some of us saw adults working and trying very hard in life to reach their goals, face life's challenges, and maintain empathic and caring close relationships, all the while managing to be emotionally mature and stable. But their lives and relationships did not turn out as they had hoped and planned. This could have led us, their children, to discouragement, cynicism, and a decision to not try so hard because "it doesn't pay off anyway." Or we may have seen that misfortune can occur in anyone's life and we forged ahead with optimism and determination—important aspects of EQ.

One of the most powerful influences in your life is how your parents related to each other. You are fortunate if your chief role models for marriage had a healthy relationship. Even if they did not, you can learn how to do this now. To determine if your parents used EQ in their marriage, stop and ask yourself if they:

- ° Listened to each other attentively

- ° Tuned in to and tried to understand each other

- ° Treated each other with respect

- ° Expressed their feelings openly and appropriately to each other

○ Showed empathy and compassion for each other's feelings or life experiences

○ Managed their conflicts appropriately

○ Displayed patience with each other

○ Persisted and worked through their hard times

○ Displayed personal power as individuals

○ Were both self-motivated

○ Were not always determined to have their own way

○ Appeared to be positive and hopeful about life and their relationship

○ Seemed to know themselves pretty well

We do repeat our parents' patterns, and this modeling can be positive or negative. Some of us insist that we will "never be like our parents" or we claim we want to "have a marriage like Mom and Dad had." An important reminder: the purpose of this examination of your parents' marriage is not to find fault and blame. It is just another key to self-awareness and self-understanding!

Another common issue to look at is the presence of alcoholism or any other serious addictions or dependencies. Addiction is a family disease not the disease of an individual. Inevitably, unhealthy emotional and behavioral patterns show up in families when one or both parents are alcoholic or substance dependent. If you are an adult child of an alcoholic, examining the following list may be helpful.

Which of these do you recall seeing in the influential person(s) who were addicted to alcohol or drugs?

○ Inappropriate acting out

○ Impulsivity

○ Intolerance and impatience

○ Lack of motivation or ambition

- ○ Giving up easily

- ○ Blaming others for difficulties

- ○ Hopelessness

- ○ Insensitivity or obliviousness to the feelings of others

- ○ Unpredictability

- ○ Lack of attunement or erratic behavior

- ○ Fear and distrust

- ○ Excessive anger

- ○ Verbal or physical abuse

Study these lists carefully and try to determine how any of these have affected you as an adult. Nearly every one of them is an antithesis to EQ. Keeping a journal or simply recalling experiences and sharing them with your partner helps you to understand yourself and can open the door for greater attunement and bonding between the two of you.

If you indeed have put yourself under a microscope as suggested, you are well on your way to understanding the roots of your EQ.

OBSERVE OTHERS AND YOURSELF

If you have done all you can to understand the influence of your past on the present, you may be eager to take this next step.

We utilize one aspect of our EQ to develop another.

You can learn a lot by carefully observing yourself and the people with whom you interact. Watch the behaviors of your family, friends, and coworkers very closely; listen carefully to what they say and how they say it; notice how they express feelings; track their nuances; etc. Do the same for yourself. Carry a note pad, Palm Pilot, or recorder; observe these behaviors over a period of several months. This may sound like a daunting task, but it can be fun. It requires other qualities of EQ—most notably, the ability of attunement or tuning in to others and yourself. You will encounter very confident, successful people who have no idea how they affect others—in either a positive or negative way. This indicates that they have not developed this component of EQ.

While a certain amount of self-awareness and other aspects of EQ can be developed on your own, some of this requires the involvement of other people. The presence of others is often an indispensable resource in your process.

Friends are a rich resource if they are willing and able to provide honest feedback to you. Family members often know you best and can call on you to be your best or point out things of which you are unaware. Unfortunately, some families cannot or will not provide helpful feedback. Others, such as people you know through work, church, or your neighborhood, can help with your EQ development depending upon the depth of your relationship and whether their feedback is appropriate. And ideally the most valuable resource is having a spouse, partner, or "buddy" who is consciously committed to taking this journey with you.

Use the checklist below to get started in self-observation. It includes both negative and positive qualities or attitudes.

Do I display these?

○ **Compassion for others**

○ **Ability to be attuned to those around me**

○ **Tolerance**

○ **Impatience**

○ **Ability to delay gratification or to handle defeat**

○ **Lack of self-motivation**

○ **Ability to use and modulate my emotions appropriately**

○ **Lack of belief in myself**

○ **Sense of hope and optimism**

Now construct your own personal inventory about how you see yourself and how you think you come across and are seen by others.

Here are some other things to consider about your behavior and feelings.

○ **Are you angry a lot or do others perceive you as angry?**

○ **Are you generally positive and optimistic?**

○ Pay attention to whether you can identify what you are feeling most of the time. Do you honor those feelings?

○ Pay attention to how well you listen to those around you. Do others feel heard by you?

○ Ask yourself if you are truly tuned in to your partner.

○ Notice how much empathy you feel for him/her.

○ How do you show compassion for your partner?

○ Watch how well you manage your feelings as required by different situations.

○ How do others perceive you emotionally?

○ Find out if those close to you see you as:

Emotionally stable ___ Unstable ___ Volatile ___
Overreactive ___ Shut down ___

○ Pay attention to whether your thoughts about people, life, and daily circumstances are more negative or positive.

○ Notice if your thoughts and feelings about the future are more hopeful or hopeless—optimistic or pessimistic, respectively.

○ Keep track of how you react when things go wrong or you are having difficulty in your life. What do others see?

○ Do you "freak out" and "lose it" when faced with obstacles or are you calm and confident? Do you continue to function as necessary?

○ Are you a leader?

○ Look at your experiences of failures or the mistakes you have made. How have you handled these?

○ What have your successes and failures taught you about yourself?

- Notice whether you are critical and judgmental of others or supportive of them.

- Do you see yourself as superior or equal to others?

- Pay close attention to how powerful or powerless you feel in your relationship, at work, with friends, and in other areas of life.

- Are you in charge of your own outcomes? Or do you feel more like a victim?

- Notice how you react when you really want something and cannot have it.

- Pay close attention to how you respond to your impulses and desires.

After you evaluate yourself using this inventory, ask your closest friends and family to use it to evaluate you and give you feedback. Ask them to be totally honest. There are thousands of things we could look at in trying to understand how we are seen by others. But our focus here is on those qualities that relate specifically to EQ.

These questions are just suggestions. Design and use an inventory for yourself, and then adjust and use it with friends and family. Now it's your partner's turn to give you feedback on these items. Relax and try to be open and receptive. If you only learn two or three things about yourself, declare this a success.

When you are trying to observe yourself and others, it can be very effective to have a symbolic or tangible reminder available. The old "rubber band on the wrist" is a good example. Many recovering alcoholics carry a special coin in their pockets. You may consider keeping a small, smooth rock handy or wear a special ring or other piece of jewelry.

Having your own special code word to say or listen for can be helpful, as well as carrying a small laminated card listing coaching or reminder points. It may lighten things up between you and your mate if you fashion a "magic wand" out of a pencil or dowel and keep it handy to use as a reminder when things get tense or difficult. Think of something that might work for you to help keep you on track.

TAKE PERSONALITY TESTS OR PROFILES

Other resources that can help you better understand yourself are personality inventories and personal assessment tests. The most valid tests are administered by professionals and include such widely used instruments as the Myers-Briggs Type Inventory, which measures your personality type, or the more complex psychological tools such as the Minnesota Multiphasic Personality Inventory and the California Psychological Inventory. Some of these tests or profiles are only for the purpose of helping you understand yourself; others are for diagnostic purposes. You may need guidance in which tests to request depending on whether you just want to understand yourself better or whether you feel there is something "wrong" that needs to be diagnosed or identified.

How you measure or evaluate your personality depends on what it is you are trying to understand and also on the perspective of the test maker. Depending upon how serious you are about understanding yourself, you may want to know which school of thought is behind the assessment instrument you are using. If you want to be scientifically accurate, you will need to use a test that has both statistical reliability and validity.

There are literally hundreds of such tools available, and nearly every aspect of your personality is measurable. If you read popular literature, you may have noticed that many magazine articles and books contain short tests and self-assessment quizzes on different aspects of your personality or interactions with others. While many of those found in popular literature may be unscientific, they can be helpful by awakening or reawakening something about yourself.

If you are trying to increase your self-awareness through personality testing or assessment, keep in mind that some of your personality and style is determined by your genetic predisposition, i.e., it comes from your biological heritage. The rest of your personality and style is developed through your early life experiences and your natural developmental process. And then a smaller percentage is the result of your own unique physiology—your body and how it functions. Some experts claim it is about 50/50 (nature vs. nurture). Others claim that the early life experiences and developmental process contribute about 80% to whom you are today.

If you choose to apply a spiritual perspective, you can factor in that your personality and the way you function are also determined by a supreme being.

Regardless of how they are formed, your personality and style can be assessed. They are not totally fixed and can change to some degree over time through learning, effort, treatment, or growth and maturity.

ENGAGE IN BIBLIOTHERAPY

As is true for seeking professional help, bibliotherapy (reading books, articles, pamphlets, internet information, etc.) can be useful for self-awareness, self-understanding, and other aspects of EQ. Bibliotherapy can also be called "psychoeducation." Bibliotherapy has proven to be enormously effective for thousands of us who find the right resource.

Reading alone does not always lead to the level of healing or growth that you are seeking and does not guarantee success in your life or in your relationship/marriage. But virtually thousands of astute individuals report "life-changing" results from reading and actualizing what they learn from books, articles, tapes, and internet information that is pertinent to their goals. Yes, you can improve your EQ and the way you live your life by reading.

In this culture, which is committed to self-improvement, bibliotherapy is probably the most popular form of "self-help." Our information-rich culture helps us understand ourselves and improve our relationships and contributes to various aspects of our mental and physical health as well as to personal

Keep in mind as you benefit from reading that the most effective way to develop emotional maturity and intelligence is through practice and interaction with others.

and professional growth. A word of caution—some of the resources available to the public are "junk" and worse, potentially dangerous. It is wise for you to look at the credibility of the author or to consult with a professional when searching for resources designed to help you understand yourself, make major changes, or improve your love relationship.

The Bibliography includes resources that provide insight; give you "how tos" and guidelines for specific changes; can help you heal; or function as workbooks containing hands-on or experiential tasks and exercises. Most can be used in conjunction with some form of psychotherapy or group process.

PARTICIPATE IN HEALING OR PERSONAL GROWTH WORKSHOPS AND SEMINARS

This is another form of self-help that has swept the nation in recent decades and can also be considered "psychoeducational." There is a proliferation of motivational seminars in the workplace that address the use of EQ for career enhancement, improving sales abilities, and other profit-motive endeavors. Some of this may be applicable to your personal life for such things as communication skills or conflict management. However, there are significant differences between how you function in the workplace and how you behave in your personal, intimate relationships. This leaves a clear need for workshops and seminars that focus specifically on helping you increase your self-awareness and other aspects of EQ for personal, intimate relating. There just aren't many available.

Churches sometimes offer such groups and might put a particular doctrinaire spin on what is taught or experienced. Regardless of the setting, an advantage of attending is that most EQ is built on interactions with others. Workshops, seminars, and classes, if structured appropriately, can provide you with valuable face-to-face interactions and opportunities for feedback. An extensive training program or support group or a one- to two-day workshop (such as an intensive weekend retreat) have shown remarkable results.

One new form of self-help, which bridges the seminar and group therapy formats, is that of online support groups through the internet. These provide you with educational materials as well as dialogue with your peers who are also trying to understand themselves better. Again, a caution—it may be advisable to seek the guidance of a professional while using such a service due to the potential danger posed by "crackpots" who have access to the internet. Keep in mind that this type of learning and growth is incomplete because it lacks the face-to-face contact that is essential for the full development of self-awareness.

FIND A GOOD THERAPIST

One of the best ways to get to know and understand yourself is through individual, couple, or group therapy. While it can be difficult to find a therapist who is a good "fit" for you and/or your relationship, don't underestimate the value of this process. If you have not had a good experience with this in the past, don't give up. Get a referral from a friend or family member. The therapy process has historically proven to be one of the most effective resources for self-understanding.

WORDS OF WISDOM AND WARNINGS

Perhaps you have experienced some of the obstacles mentioned in this chapter and nonetheless have the dogged determination to overcome them. Remarkably, despite any maltreatment, neglect, poor role modeling, or trauma, you may have the natural ability to determine that you are going to push yourself to emotional maturity, life success, and healthy relationships. Good for you!

A caveat: This is admirable as long as it is not driven by a poisonous or vindictive motivation or that rascally "people-pleasing" motive. It is best if this resilience is intrinsically and positively motivated. Be careful not to overlook your deficits by excusing or denying your heritage. Pay attention to whether you are still angrily blaming your past.

You can also get caught up in excusing your parents' behavior or treatment of you with "they did the best they could" or "I understand why they were the way they were." This can sidetrack your own self-understanding. Do your work first and then get to forgiveness and recognizing that they too were hindered. But don't put the cart before the horse!

Some of us use our early experiences and natural abilities to become highly successful in our careers but remain emotionally inept and have difficulty being truly close to our loved ones, including our love partners. Successful individuals are often "married" to their careers while their close personal connections are virtually nonexistent. If this is true for you, do yourself and your partner a favor by making your relationship as much a priority as your career.

Take this investigative journey into what led to your emotional strengths or deficits. Ask yourself, "What and how did I learn about close love relationships that is influencing my relationship/marriage today?"

Life in general brings with it frustration, setbacks, and defeats; those of you who learned to handle these obstacles at an early age may find it easier to be emotionally intelligent now and thus be good candidates for healthy relationships. Clearly, marriage and other committed relationships are difficult at best, and we cannot hope for one that is problem free. There is truth in the old adage that "adversity builds character."

This chapter suggested resources for developing your self-awareness—the cornerstone for all other components of EQ. Through some combination of tests or profiles, self-observation and feedback from others, examining your personal history and early life experience, seeking help from a mental health professional, using bibliotherapy resources, and participating in groups, you can get to really know yourself and how you relate to others (particularly your partner).

•   •   •

So you see yourself more clearly now. That's good. You are ready to move on to Chapter 10, where the focus is on developing the most important aspect of relating to your partner—your feelings or emotions and theirs.

CHAPTER TEN

Understanding and Expressing Your Emotions

There can be no transforming of darkness into light
and of apathy into movement without emotion.

—CARL JUNG, M.D.

What are you feeling at the moment? What about five minutes ago? What caused those feelings? These are not always easy questions to answer. Your emotions are a hugely important part of who you are as a human being. They help you cope with life, but what is most important for our purposes here is that they help you connect and relate effectively with your partner.

As you learn to access, identify, regulate, and express your emotions, you will find that this is another aspect of knowing and understanding yourself. Becoming really good at it does improve with experience, but it is a lifelong process. Most of us never perfect it.

FAMILIARIZE YOURSELF WITH THE LANGUAGE OF EMOTION: THE FEELING WORDS

It is common to have a narrow or incomplete sense of what feelings are even possible. You can learn to identify and name a wider variety of emotions over time and through experience if you are willing to expand your knowledge of emotion. You can respond appropriately to specific situations rather than with an off the cuff reaction if you have a more personalized understanding of your emotions.

An example of this might be to react to something your partner does with bewilderment instead of reaching for the immediate and easy feeling of anger. Another example might be to respond to something with caution instead of crippling fear.

Improving this aspect of your emotional intelligence (EQ) requires the help of your partner or other people. There is disagreement about how to define the term *emotion* in a straightforward way because emotions are involved in several levels of your everyday functioning: your feelings, biological reactions, desires or motivations, and social interactions. These and perhaps other dimensions represent the rather broad character of a word we use all the time but cannot narrowly define.

There is also disagreement among the experts in this field on how many emotions there are and which are the primary or most important ones. I will suggest some primary emotions and then provide you with a list of "feeling words" with which to work. It is helpful to make a copy of this list and keep it handy to use as a tool as you work to develop this EQ skill—getting in touch with and expressing your emotions.

The primary emotions considered here are fear, anger, joy/happiness, and sadness. Among others that are important but not broken down into feeling words in the list below are interest/eagerness, guilt, shame, disgust, and hurt. (To those of you who are hopeless romantics, please note that the word *love* is not an emotion!)

Fear	Anger	Joy/Happiness	Sadness
Apprehensive	Resentful	Contented	Melancholy
Anxious	Indignant	Satisfied	Flat/blah
Alarmed	Bitter	Peaceful/secure	Discontented
Insecure	Grumpy	Playful	Sympathetic
Suspicious	Belligerent	Ecstatic	Compassionate
Worried	Sullen	Pleased	Sorrowful
Feeling threatened	Impatient	Cheerful	Sulky
Panicked	Offended	Lighthearted	Depressed
Overly cautious	Blaming	Optimistic	Discouraged
Dependent	Stubborn	Vivacious	Worthless

ACCESS AND IDENTIFY YOUR FEELINGS

The next step in this process is to try to identify what you are feeling at any point in time. And for some of us this is quite difficult! Once you can identify and name what you are feeling, managing and expressing it is a key to functioning with EQ.

Do you sometimes notice that you have a vague awareness of an emotional state, but you don't know what it is? Or do you misidentify a feeling or mask it with another? This is often the experience with anger. We frequently feel fear or sadness but express these emotions as anger. Another problem is not recognizing that your feelings can vary greatly in their intensity and that you can experience more than one feeling at the same time.

It is common to have only a fuzzy awareness of what you are truly feeling and therefore be unable to express it effectively. If you have a condition known as alexithymia, you may truly have no idea what you feel and are totally unable to read the emotional states of others. This can also be true of certain types of autism and Asperger syndrome. As you might imagine, people with this disorder are enormously frustrating to their mates or close associates.

Earlier I briefly described the various brain centers that affect the generation and expression of your emotions. While your feelings may originate in the more primitive portions of your brain, to identify and express them requires the more evolved areas that regulate the processes of thinking and reasoning. Through proper training, you can learn to identify your feelings with accuracy, express them effectively, and read the feelings of others. The latter ability is a real gift to your love partner.

This training usually requires interaction with someone who is eager to help you develop this "emotional competence" and is invested in learning it for themselves as well.

Most of us long to love, be loved, and to experience deep feeling and intimate connection. However, these achievements are difficult, if not impossible, if we lack emotional awareness or the ability to express what we feel. We also long to have a sense of personal power and freedom in our lives but may be unaware that these experiences lead to a feeling of deep connection as well.

There are very few environments or areas of life that allow for the unbridled expression of whatever you are feeling. We all want to scream "f___ off" at times or wail uncontrollably but can't in most circumstances. Does having this quality of EQ require you to be emotionally repressed, stoic, or flat? Not at all. Management and appropriate use of emotions are not the same as being stifled. People often boast that they are able to successfully "control their anger." "Control" is not the same as management or regulation and may actually cause damage to your physical and mental health. When we know what we feel, accept and are comfortable with our feelings, and act on them constructively, we are physically and mentally healthier and have healthier relationships.

Western society tends to value intellect over emotion and teaches that to succeed in life we must be rational and objective, not emotional or feeling. Jeanne Segal, Ph.D., psychologist and author of *Raising Your Emotional Intelligence*, finds that " . . . when we let ourselves feel our emotions fully and physically, as we're designed to do, we tap into parts of the brain that have been lying dormant and gain the potential for keeping our intelligence growing for life."[27]

There is a synergy between your intelligence quotient and your EQ—one without the other is incomplete or ineffectual, and each contributes to the other. Have you been exposed to ideas such as: being emotional is unwise or dangerous, emotion is inferior to reason, you must use self-control to stifle your feelings, and emotion in general can cloud your judgment? If you adopt this way of thinking, you may be uncomfortable with being emotionally vulnerable and "exposed"; yet this is the very thing that paves the way for the closeness you desire.

The centers throughout your brain that involve emotion wield significant power over all brain function, including your intellect. It is in keeping the lines of communication open between the limbic system and neocortex that compassion, empathy, self-management, and other EQ qualities can be developed and can contribute to rational thought.

So how do you access and identify your feelings?

Tune In to Your Body

One key way of achieving this is to tune in to your body. Your emotions are physically based as these common phrases illustrate:

- "I had a gut feeling about this."

- "This just breaks my heart."

- "This (person or situation) is a pain in the neck."

- "That made my skin crawl."

- "My heart was in my throat."

- "That really chokes me up."

- "I was so angry that I was ready to burst."

- "That sent chills up my spine."

- "This situation just makes me sick."

- "I was so excited that I couldn't eat."

- "I am going to trust my gut."

- "I put my foot in my mouth."

- "I turned beet red."

Research supports the notion that your emotions are held in your body. You can learn to access them by paying closer attention to your body. Like most people, you may get so caught up in life that you forget about your body. To use it for emotional information, remind yourself as often as possible throughout the day to slow down and focus on what you are feeling physically.

○ Are your muscles relaxed or tense?

○ Is your breathing deep or shallow?

○ Is there stiffness in your neck or shoulders?

○ What is going on in your stomach? Your heart?

○ Are you relaxed or scowling and wrinkling your brow?

○ Do you smile a lot?

○ Do you relax your hands or often clench your fists?

○ Do you drum your fingers on your desk?

○ Do you bite your nails?

○ Notice when your perspiring increases/decreases.

○ Pay attention to your posture. Do you feel different when you slouch? When you stand up straight?

○ What body sensations do you notice when you hear loud noises, a baby cry, etc.?

○ Where do you feel it in your body when you have to slow down and "put on your brakes"?

○ What happens to your body when you get or give a loved one a long warm hug?

Each of these is obviously a physical reaction to what you are feeling. You can train yourself to stop, "check in" several times throughout the day, and concentrate on changing to more relaxed, healthy responses. This puts you in touch with your emotions.

Get Feedback

One of the best ways to learn to understand your emotions is to have others around who can and will give you honest feedback. Obviously the ideal situation is to have your committed partner be your "feedback buddy." Even if you have such a person in your life, the two of you are likely to need guidance and training in the process of how to identify and maneuver your way through your feelings. We need experience and practice with others to achieve the level of emotional sophistication that a healthy relationship requires.

If you are at a primitive state in your emotional awareness and often "read" yourself or your partner inaccurately, there is still hope! Emotional awareness and expression can be learned, but there is no quick and easy way to achieve it.

Try the following: Talk to a friend or mate on a regular basis about your feelings and invite them to do the same. Ask them to give you honest feedback about which emotions you display and to offer a critique or probe with questions. For example, perhaps you appear angry a lot or anger is the only emotion you express. Maybe you come across as defensive or anxious or you may be told that you appear peaceful and secure.

You and your "feedback buddy" can also use the primary emotions chart on page 169 as a tool to facilitate discussions about the emotions that come up for you. Remember at this stage to focus mostly on identifying and not so much on expressing. How often do you have the opportunity to get honest, constructive feedback from someone on such a personal level? At work, you may get feedback in performance evaluations—but rarely in your private life does someone tell you how you come across emotionally.

Relax and Center Yourself

The following exercise is guaranteed to help you access and become more familiar with your emotions. Warning: Unexpected and potentially uncomfortable feelings may emerge. This is not for the faint of heart when it comes to allowing yourself to feel!

Step One: Completely *stop* what you are doing several times during the day. This may involve taking breaks at work or practicing first in the evening or on weekends. But you must completely *stop*. I sometimes encourage people to "just stop the world."

Step Two: Close your eyes anad take three or four deep, cleansing breaths, breathing in through your nose and out through your mouth. You can do nothing else (sneeze, cough, laugh, cry) when you are breathing deeply in this fashion. If you have a physiological or health problem that makes this difficult, modify it accordingly.

Step Three: Relax your entire body as much as possible. This may be difficult at work. During the workday perhaps you will need to go out to your car or into an empty lounge with a lock on the door. At home find an isolated quiet place. It is ideal if you can relax your entire body, beginning with your feet and moving upward to your neck and head. First tense each part of your body, and then let each part go limp. Tighten. Relax. Tighten. Relax.

Step Four: Now shift your focus inside—to your "center." If you have never done anything that has familiarized you with the idea of centering, you may need to look into this idea ahead of time. You can think of this as the center of your being or your soul. But remember that the body is the seat of emotions, and so you may find your center by focusing your attention in your chest, solar plexus, abdomen, or . . . ? Where you feel the center of your being is unique to you as an individual.

Step Five: Ask yourself what you are feeling at the moment, what you felt at a specific time earlier that day, what you feel about a particular person or event, or what you are feeling about something coming up in the future. You may need to use the list of feelings listed on page 169. Stay with this awareness for a few moments. Stay relaxed as you name the feeling(s).

Step Six: Slowly open your eyes and return to a more fully conscious state.

Step Seven: Write down what emotions came up for you. This can be unsettling at times but can lead to a very positive experience.

Step Eight: When the time or situation is right, speak about your feelings to someone with whom you feel safe or comfortable or take the actions you need to take based on the feelings that emerged. Ideally, this safe person will be your partner.

For those of you who easily access and identify your feelings, this exercise may not be necessary. If you do need it, remember to do it as many times during the day as possible for several weeks. This exercise can also help uncover feelings with which you have been out of touch.

Journal

Think of journaling in a broad sense. You might want to write intensively several pages at a time or record just a few random words or notes. Journaling does not imply pen and paper only. You may choose to use your computer, a recorder, a day-timer, a calendar, or a Palm Pilot. Your purpose is to access, identify, and record feelings. You will need to stop, relax, and focus as you do this. In whatever fashion fits you, record what you are feeling at the moment or how you felt about a particular situation at a recent time.

Be consistent for several weeks or perhaps longer if you need additional work in accessing and identifying your emotions. If you prefer not to keep a record, commit to yourself that you will "mentally record" by focusing attention on your emotions throughout the day for an extended period of time.

EXAMINE HOW YOU MANAGE, EXPRESS, AND USE YOUR EMOTIONS

Now that you have learned some ways to access and identify your feelings, it's time to move on to expression. Sometimes your emotions just come out of the blue, and you cannot manage them until you have time to focus and think. Imagine encountering a snake on a path while you are walking. You would have an immediate biologically induced emotion—fear! If you have received a call informing you that a loved one has unexpectedly died, you experience sudden shock and sadness. In addition to being felt in your body, such strong feelings are governed by your thoughts and beliefs.

Your feelings are often the result of your thoughts. It is your appraisal or evaluation of a situation that causes a particular feeling and not always the situation itself. You and your partner can have the same experience but respond to it with different feelings. Some of this may be gender related, due to different biological responses, or the result of your personality types. But even these factors are connected to the thought processes you have learned or chosen to use.

Try the following exercise:

- For approximately two weeks pay close attention to your interactions with your mate, his/her behaviors, and situations involving both of you.

- First, track your thoughts and your way of appraising or viewing what has occurred.

- As much as possible, write down or somehow keep track of these thoughts, appraisals, and views.

- At the same time keep the list of feelings handy that are listed on page 169. Identify which feelings emerge with your thoughts.

You are likely to find that if you choose to view something in your relationship in a positive way, your feelings are more likely to be pleasant. If you have a negative appraisal, you are more likely to have a less than positive feeling.

Continue to do this until you see how much your thoughts affect your feelings.

If you doubt that you can learn to manage and express your feelings, think about others you know who have learned to do it. They could be your role models. You may know someone personally or you may be able to witness this in certain professions that have to maintain neutrality. These professions may include teachers, medical personnel, police or fire workers, flight attendants, or mental health professionals. You may say that this is just a workplace mask. And in some cases it may be. But such learning is possible for you as well, and it can be translated from your professional to your personal life.

Needless to say, managing your emotions is a core ability in a close, loving relationship. Some experts claim that the degree to which you feel your emotions, or "affect intensity" as it is technically called, has a biological basis. In other words, it is a natural part of who we are. Those who feel emotions very strongly and express them with reactivity are seen as being "affect intense." Those who experience and express their emotions mildly are called "affect stable." Regardless of whether our emotional style is natural to us or has been learned, we all need to learn to manage it and express ourselves in an appropriate or constructive manner.

The bottom line is that just as identifying your emotions requires you to stop and focus, even more important is to do so before expressing them. The first step in managing and expressing is to use the *stop*, *breathe*, and *center* exercise. At the proper time in this process think of something appropriate to say or do in a situation or interaction. For our purposes here, try to apply this mostly to your love partner. You can easily see why this requires self-awareness.

For most of us, this takes a lot of practice. So often when we feel an emotion, especially a strong one, our tendency is to just spontaneously express it, cry, or act out! And this applies to positive emotions as well as negative. It is not always appropriate to walk up to someone and say we love them or to express unfettered joy in certain circumstances. Don't forget: whether we like it or not, we are judged or evaluated by how we express our emotions, and how we do this affects other people! It all reflects our level of maturity and EQ.

The one emotion that many of us have difficulty managing and expressing appropriately is anger.

If you have a serious problem in handling your anger, regardless of the cause, it may be advisable for you to participate in an anger management course. Conversely, you may be completely stifled with your anger and never express it.

If you want to be emotionally intelligent in your relationship, the first thing to do when you are angry is to *stop*. Give yourself time to think before you act or speak. Even if your partner does something like criticize you unfairly, simply stop and think before you respond. Just as when you are drunk, if you are angry, you are in an altered state of consciousness. None of us can act or speak appropriately when we are "altered."

When you are angry in your relationship, you are not likely to be very insightful; you may interpret the actions or behaviors of your partner in a negative light; and you tend to project things onto your partner that don't belong to them. When you practice the technique of stopping, calming down, and thinking more clearly, evaluate these:

- **Your level of insight.**

- **Your negative interpretations.**

- **How much you are projecting.**

- **What did you find?**

- **What did you learn about yourself?**

- **What did you learn about your partner?**

The most effective way to handle anger in a relationship/marriage is to learn cooperative interaction or dialogue skills. Depending on your history with these skills, you may have to relearn how to express anger and other emotions. These appropriate skills are described at various points throughout this book. Practice them over and over again.

Do not be seduced by those who claim that the best thing to do with anger is to just ventilate it—just spew it out! This is not a good idea. It does not reflect EQ or maturity, and it is harmful to marriage. Some people advocate a "tell it like it is" philosophy in personal interactions. This is only effective if it is used in a careful, well thought out manner which shows respect and concern for your listener. Many people who live by the "tell it like it is" philosophy use this as an excuse to be insensitive and mean!

As you are practicing the appropriate expression of emotions, remind yourself that the way you handle your emotions has a powerful effect on your health and on the health of those around you. For example, constant fighting and conflict are definitely toxic to the body. They can also be toxic to those around you, especially children.

Have you ever wondered what is appropriate regarding the frequency of anger in a marriage? A good rule of thumb in a healthy relationship is to not have more than one very angry exchange per month. Anger is a normal and necessary emotion, but it can erode the attachment and love in your relationship/marriage if it is too pervasive.

In most cases an emotional exchange calls for calm, cool headedness, an open and receptive attitude, and fine-tuned communication skills. Even when you are not angry or particularly emotional, one of the most important tools to use in your interactions is the "I statement" or "I message." Remember to express only your own feelings, needs, actions, motives, or perspectives. You will be amazed at the power of speaking only for yourself and completely avoiding speaking for your partner. If you need something from your partner, express it as a positive request not as a demand or accusation.

Examples include:

- "I need to talk to you" or "Can we take some time to talk?" rather than "We need to talk."

- "I am concerned that _____ didn't get handled" instead of "You didn't do _____."

- "I feel _____ when you _____" rather than "You make me feel _____."

- "I would like it if you would _____" rather than "You should _____."

- "I need _____" rather than "You never do _____."

It is very easy to slip into projecting and blaming with your statements or messages. To learn to avoid this is more important than you may think. You come across as being willing to solve problems and work things out and not as just wanting to get your own way or engage in battle.

An "I statement or message" is open and inviting. A "You statement or message" comes across as critical, controlling, or invasive. Instead of opening the door between you and your partner, it tends to close it. You will find more information about this in any good resource on effective communication.

Avoid blaming and projecting your own negative emotions onto your partner, no matter what the circumstances. An emotionally intelligent person can do this. Try this exercise: Find time to discuss an emotion-laden issue with your partner. Choose an easy issue first, and then move on to one that is more "loaded."

1. Identify your feeling as described on page 169.

2. Express this feeling with an "I statement." Don't hold back.

3. Speak what it is you are feeling in a straightforward way.

4. Wait for your partner's response.

5. Keep this going in a circular fashion as long as it is working for you.

You may need to practice first with a friend, support group, or professional before you try it with your partner. Try this over and over again until you are comfortable with it. Having a cooperative receptive partner is a huge asset, but you can learn to express what you are feeling regardless of his/her level of receptivity. You can develop the emotionally intelligent way of expressing your emotions if you practice this repeatedly. Your partner may not respond in a way that shows EQ, but you should "stick to the rules" nonetheless.

If the emotions you are feeling are extremely strong, it is best to wait until you feel prepared to express them in a way that can be more easily received. Perhaps you are very sad and need to be held while you cry. This can be satisfying, but it takes two. The next EQ quality of empathy and attunement may be called for here as well.

Another essential habit for expressing your emotions is that of asking appropriate questions. This is absolutely one of the most useful tools in personal interactions.

Common examples of things you can practice asking your partner are:

- **"Can you tell me what you're feeling right now?"**

- **"Can you help me understand why you did it that way?"**

- **"What are/were you intending?"**

- **"Can you please clarify what you mean?"**

Watch your tone. These must be nondefensive or nonaccusatory questions—asked truly for inquiry and gathering information. If you look carefully at this list, you can see that each of these questions can be asked with an ugly or accusatory tone. For example: *"What* did you mean by *that"*?

Try this exercise: Write out a list of questions you could ask your partner about some of your most common issues, misunderstandings, or areas of need. Keep them handy. Use the questions as they are applicable in your interactions and then record the results. Do this over an extended period—perhaps two weeks. Remember that the goal is to express and manage emotions. What did you find?

Like all other aspects of EQ: practice, practice, practice.

Here are a couple of examples:

1. If your partner is late in arriving home, you can ask a nonaccusing question about his/her day or the drive home. "Did you have a hard day? Is that what made you late?"

2. If your partner appears to be grouchy or is snapping at you, instead of snapping back, ask a question about what they might be feeling. For example, "Is something bothering you today?" "Did I do something to upset you?"

3. If your partner has had a hurtful experience or gone through a loss, you may ask if they would be comfortable sharing their feelings of hurt or sadness with you. If they agree, do not offer advice or try to cheer them up, just *listen* to show your support and ask appropriate questions.

Remember that one way to learn to access, identify, and express your feelings is by having someone safe and nonjudgmental with whom to do it! Once you have this in your relationship, you don't want to lose it.

The other primary emotions of fear, joy, and sadness may also be stifled or inappropriately expressed in your relationship. You can modify the preceding suggestions about anger to some degree and apply them to these emotions as well. Chapter 11 offers guidelines for this by helping you with empathy and attunement.

TAKE ASSESSMENT TESTS

Assessment tools are available for measuring your ability to access and express your emotions. I would recommend Claude Steiner's emotional awareness questionnaire and emotional awareness scale, listed in the Bibliography. You may choose to search for emotional expressivity scales, which help you to determine how strongly you express your emotions.

Once you have measured, either formally or informally, the degree and style of your emotional expressivity, you can monitor it in yourself and either continue status quo or increase or change it. This may even require you to "force" yourself to express your feelings more openly. Warning: Be sure you review appropriateness of expression. For some of us, our common sense can guide us in what is the appropriate way to express and identify what we are feeling. But a large number of people are incompetent in this important area of EQ.

Do you really know when and how to express your anger appropriately? Joy and excitement? Sadness? Fondness or love? Compassion?

If you can locate and take an emotional awareness or expressivity scale, think about the results. Then keep track of how these test results seem to fit with what you observe about yourself.

SUMMARY

Learning feeling words, tuning in to your body, getting feedback, using relax and center exercises, journaling, and practicing good communication can help you to access, identify, and express your feelings.

We are all different and need to experiment to determine what works for us. For example, if you decide to get professional help, remember that some people respond better to body-centered psychotherapies and others to in-depth talk style. For still others, a combination of both is best. The same can be said for any of the techniques you do on your own as outlined in this chapter. You will eventually determine what is best for you.

In general, the more you express your feelings (in an appropriate manner, of course), the more success you will have in committed love relationships. Such expression is also good for your psychological health.

•   •   •

No matter how "tough" and independent you are, at some level you want your partner to be in touch with you at more than a superficial level, to really try to understand you, and to be able to offer empathy or compassion when you need it.

Chapter 11 paves the way for this oh-so-welcome component.

Empathizing and Being Attuned to Your Love Partner

Empathy—the human echo—is the indispensable stuff of emotional well-being.

—MIKE NICHOLS, PH.D., IN *THE LOST ART OF LISTENING*

Who wouldn't want a partner to be tuned in to them and understand their needs and feelings? Someone who would listen and be interested or compassionate? To most of us, this quality is highly valued in a mate.

If you do not have or cannot develop the ability to tune into your partner and experience empathy for him/her, do not count on having a satisfying relationship. We cannot overemphasize the importance of empathy and attunement in marriage and other social relationships. Goleman refers to empathy as the "fundamental people skill." It leads to compassion, one of the cornerstones in the foundation of every good relationship.

As you proceed to develop or strengthen this quality, keep in mind that if you stay attuned to your own feelings, having empathy for your partner will come more easily. Also, pay attention to the progression—self-awareness leads to being tuned in to your partner and attunement leads to empathy, which in turn leads to the ability to be compassionate and the reward of greater relationship satisfaction.

EARLY TRAINING IN EMPATHY

We are all born with the capacity to be empathic and attuned to others. This can get contaminated or enhanced and refined by our upbringing. (It can also be diminished by a physiologically based condition, but this is rare.) If you were raised in a family or environment that was not very empathic and did not promote emotional closeness, this may be an uphill climb for you. Other red flags in early life experience include being in a critical or judgmental environment or one which taught you that vulnerability was unsafe or unwise.

If you were treated with empathy as a child, you will have greater success showing it to yourself and others as an adult. As a first step in working on this, consider the following questions. They may help you determine how your early experience influenced your development of this aspect of emotional intelli-

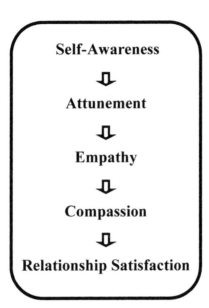

Figure 11-1

gence (EQ). This is a good place to record some of your memories as you answer these questions.

- Did your parents or family listen to you carefully when you were a child?

- Did they seem to notice when you were having strong feelings about something?

- Did they respond to your tears, anger, fear, or laughter in a way that felt affirming?

- Did they try to "shush" or demean your strong emotions?

- Did you get the feeling that your parents were truly interested in you and your life?

- Did they support your activities/interests by attending events in which you participated?

- If you were really upset, did your parents try to comfort you or just tell you to "get over it?"

- Were you taught in your family to care about others and their feelings—either inside or outside the family?

- Did it appear to you that your parents were tuned in to each other and to your siblings?

- Did they treat each other with empathy or compassion?

ASSESS YOUR CURRENT LEVEL OF EMPATHY AND COMPASSION

There is no question that empathy puts us in touch with the experiences and feelings of others, whether they are strangers or people close to us. None of us wants to see ourselves or be seen by others as heartless, but it is essential that you know this part of yourself. Answer the questions listed below as honestly as possible.

Which stories or images that you see on TV or read about in the daily news stir emotion in you? For example:

- Abused children?

- Refugees?

- Neglected elderly?

- Mistreated animals?

- Poverty or starvation?

- Victims of disaster?

- Displays of bigotry or discrimination?

- War or military skirmishes?

- Others? _____
  What feelings emerge? (besides anger) _____

How do you feel (besides angry) in the following situations that you may encounter in your daily life?

- A parent being harsh with a child? _____

- A person who is clearly mentally or physically impaired? _____

- Someone who appears to be either drunk or on drugs? _____

- A street beggar? _____

- An adult couple in a loud argument? _____

- An individual being demeaned by another such as in a consumer–salesperson or a husband–wife interaction? _____

- An overweight person? _____

- Someone whose car has broken down alongside the highway? _____

- When your child or a child you are with injures him/herself? _____

- When an adult you are with injures him/herself? _____

- If a friend or associate reports to you that they have just been fired from a job they really enjoy? _____

- If a friend or associate reports to you that someone close to them has just died? _____

- When you see a woman whom you know crying openly? _____

- When you see a man whom you know crying openly? _____

- When you see your husband or wife crying openly? _____

- When you sense that your love partner is going through a difficult time? _____

If you are honest in answering these questions, you can get a fairly accurate sense of your level of empathy or compassion. If you cannot and doing this is foreign to you, discuss these items and your reaction to them with your partner, a "safe" friend, or a professional.

GET OVER YOURSELF!

While "get over yourself" is a popular slang expression, it conveys wisdom. To get outside yourself and overcome your self-absorption is essential for being tuned into another person.

We may all encounter people who see everything as being about him/herself or in some way revolving around them. They cannot get outside their own feelings and inside others' feelings, experiences, or perspectives, including those of their partner. It's cute to see a toddler in a t-shirt that says, "It's all about me." But it's not so cute on an adult! And it's actually not a good thing to teach children.

If you tend to be self-absorbed, recognizing this in yourself and how you came to be this way may be half the battle. The more you understand yourself and how you come across to others, the more attuned you can be to the feelings of your partner.

Research shows that getting outside yourself to an appropriate degree (not total self-denial) will benefit you in many ways. You are more likely to be:

- Mentally healthy

- Generally interested in others

- Socially skilled and not just entertaining to be around

- Comfortable being openly loving

- Capable of maintaining close or deep friendships

- Successful in romance and a love relationship

- A person of greater morality and integrity

While it may appear to be almost oxymoronic to ask a self-absorbed person to be appropriately self-aware, nothing is impossible. If you tend to think the world revolves around you and tend to make everything about you, the task of being attuned to others, including your partner, will just be more difficult. Empathy and compassion may be hard to achieve, but if you truly desire to be a more emotionally intelligent person and create a healthier relationship, you can do it. It may take a lifetime but so do many other valuable things in the human experience.

LEARN TO LISTEN

The most important ingredient in empathy and attunement is the ability to genuinely and effectively listen. A good way to begin to develop this EQ quality is to evaluate your ability to listen. You may want to ask friends, family members, and coworkers to give you feedback on how well you listen to them. Ask them to be honest with you. Tell them you are trying to develop more EQ in this area and their feedback is valuable to you. Do this several times! Try it over a period of time, perhaps several months.

Most importantly for our purposes here is that you listen to your partner. Therefore, ask him/her for feedback as well. When you ask for feedback, your partner must see you as someone with whom it is safe to be honest. If you respond with defensiveness, hurt, or denial, the feedback will be useless because your partner will not feel safe in sharing with you.

There are fewer things more hurtful in our life experience than not being really heard and understood by those who claim to care about us or love us. As children, being listened to makes us feel worthwhile, secure, and self-confident. We also long to be understood, but there is no way to understand unless you truly listen. Listening is loving! We sustain our relationships by listening to each other. If you listen effectively, you are temporarily setting aside your own needs or words and honoring the other person's need for attention. This in itself is being empathic.

Let's look at some of the most important things to consider when you are learning to listen more effectively.

/

Listen with Your Eyes and Your Body

Begin listening with your eyes. Train yourself to look directly at the person who is speaking to you. If you are already a very effective listener, you may be able to stay adequately tuned in without looking directly at the person speaking to you. But the speaker probably prefers that you look at him/her when he/she is speaking, especially your mate. Try to maintain a comfortable level of eye contact throughout your conversation.

The other way you listen with your eyes is to train yourself to notice people's facial and body language. Notice your own responses when you see signs of sadness on another's face, a smile, a frown, a blush or flush in color, an angry snarl, emerging tears, or glancing away. Also notice such things as hand gestures, self-hugging, nervous movements, and your response to these body messages.

You can also listen with your own body. Lean forward when the other person is speaking. Shake your head in understanding even if you don't agree with what they are saying. Smile as appropriate and frown with concern. Make small "grunts and groans" that imply you are connecting with what they are saying such as "hmm," "ugh," or "whew." Use one-word or very minimal responses that do not interrupt their train of thought such as "I see," "wow," "really?," or "I didn't know . . . " And finally, nod or shake your head as appropriate to convey that you are being attentive.

Try this exercise: For the next couple of weeks (and then for a lifetime) pay very close attention to the facial and body language of those around you—coworkers, friends, your children, and your partner. Keep a record of the kinds of things you notice and of your reactions to this information. Does it help you feel more attuned to the people in your life? What else does this tell you about yourself? About others?

Listening with Your Ears and Your Soul

As Heitler suggests in *The Power of Two,* our ears may be more essential for a strong, healthy love relationship than our sex organs. Most of us feel that we are better listeners than we truly are. Evaluate your current listening habits by using the following checklist. Remember that there is no value in an inventory such as this if you are not totally honest with yourself. Some of these are applicable to listening to anyone. Others specifically relate to your love relationship.

When you are listening:

○ Are you able to focus your full attention on the other person?

○ Do you truly set aside your own needs and your need to speak?

○ Do you refrain from disagreeing, giving advice, or talking about your own experience?

○ Are you able to stay genuinely focused and attentive and not just pretend to listen?

○ Can you listen to criticisms of yourself?

○ Do you know when you are too tired or preoccupied to listen?

○ Can you tell the other person that you may have to wait and listen later?

○ Can you listen without excessive sympathy and exaggerated concern?

○ Do you know what it means to keep your own boundaries in place when you are listening?

○ Can you listen for feelings?

○ Do you find yourself saying, "Oh, you shouldn't feel that way?"

○ Do you find listening to feelings uncomfortable?

○ Do you find yourself getting upset when the person speaking is upset (being pulled into their feelings)?

○ Are you aware of your own hidden personal agenda when you are listening?

○ Can you refrain from overreacting to what your partner is saying?

○ Do you know how to ask appropriate probing questions to get clarity from the speaker?

○ Do you believe you listen actively or passively?

○ Do you know how to appropriately restate to the speaker what you hear them saying?

○ Can you set aside your judgment of the other person and what they are saying?

○ Can you manage your own anger or reactions enough to set them aside and listen to your partner's anger toward you?

○ Are you aware of the difference between when you are *taking* interest as opposed to just *showing* interest?

○ When you are listening to your partner, are you able to refrain from thinking you wish they would change?

○ Do you acknowledge what your partner is saying even if you disagree with it?

○ Do you think your partner would say that it is safe for them to speak the truth to you?

○ Do you try to "chew on and digest" what the other person is saying to you?

○ Can you avoid a right–wrong, win–lose attitude when your partner is speaking to you about an issue on which you disagree?

The appropriate answers to the questions in this inventory are obvious. How did you score? Were you honest with yourself? Now have your partner score him/herself and then compare notes and evaluate each other. After you have both achieved a perspective on your listening skills, go back and use this list as a working tool. In other words, pull out those that you need to work on and make a separate list, which you can keep in an obvious place. Then practice, practice, practice. This could definitely improve your ability to empathize and be attuned to each other as a couple.

Being heard means being taken seriously. It satisfies
our need . . . to feel connected to others . . . the
listener helps to confirm our common humanity.
The need to be known . . . understood and
accepted by someone who really listens is
meat and drink to the human heart.

—MIKE NICHOLS, PH.D., IN *THE LOST ART OF LISTENING*

ADDITIONAL SUGGESTIONS TO HELP YOU BE TUNED IN AND EMPATHIC IN YOUR RELATIONSHIP

Having empathy is being able to receive the feelings of another and respond in a way that shows you have understood them. Often we are afraid of our partner's feelings or thoughts and are uncomfortable with them. This is especially true if what they are expressing is about us! Practice showing your understanding and acceptance of whatever your partner is sharing by conversing with him/her about what he/she has expressed, inviting him/her to say more, and further expounding. Encourage your partner to be open about his/her feelings and set your discomfort aside if the concern is about you or something you don't necessarily want to hear. Allow free expression.

Warning: Be sincere. Don't patronize. Your partner will pick up on this. Patronizing in this way is similar to sympathizing instead of empathizing. Empathy requires you to use your feelings with someone. Sympathy is a more removed, cognitive process that may not involve your true feelings and doesn't connect you to the other person.

Empathy also involves something that runs deeper than listening and conversing—the ability to be intuitive. As long as you don't get into mind reading and telling your partner what they are feeling or thinking, you can use your intuition or sixth sense to connect with them and help them to feel cared about. You may be naturally intuitive; if not, you can develop it.

If you know and understand yourself well, you may be able to trust your intuition about your partner more confidently. But the best test of the accuracy of your intuition is to invite honest feedback from your partner. Ask them if your perceptions or hunches about them are accurate. You can ask such questions as "It appears as though you are feeling _____. Is that right?" Ideally they will be honest with you.

When the shoe is on the other foot, so to speak, and your partner is expressing his/her intuitive hunches about you, the same process applies. Practice this together again and again. You will both become more intuitively mature through this process, but honest feedback is essential. The result is a more loving connection.

Remember that empathy is having the ability to feel with someone, not for them. Be careful that you are not confusing your feelings with those of your partner. It is not being tuned in or empathic to get angry because your partner is angry or to be pulled down into depression because your partner is depressed. This is codependence. If you are trying to be sympathetic instead of empathetic, the boundaries between the two of you may become blurred or dissolved. This helps no one.

Very few of us want others to come along and solve our problems. Just be there! Don't fix things!

You may feel a certain degree of anger or indignation if your partner tells you that they have been blatantly insulted or demeaned by another person. But it is not appropriate to take on their anger. The same is true for an experience involving hurt, sadness, or fear or any other emotionally laden occurrence. If you have a tendency to want to take their feelings away or make them feel differently, you are really nurturing your own discomfort and not helping them.

Giving too much and being a martyr is not an act of nobility.

First take care of yourself. Then you are more likely to have the capacity to be caring of others. For example, concentrate on your own health through adequate sleep, proper diet, and regular exercise. Also be sure that you know what your personal boundaries and limits are and how much you can give. People pleasers are nearly always eventually exposed because they burn out, get sick, or become angry. You can learn to find a balance and to know how much you have to give to others.

There is a long-standing and ongoing debate about whether or not we are responsible for others' feelings. My position is that while we are not directly responsible for what others feel, we must be tuned in enough to discern when they are having certain feelings and must respond to them in a way that is helpful. This ability to "read" your partner without "mind reading" is a sure sign of EQ.

We are also capable, through our actions and projected attitudes, to affect others' feelings. We can, for example, through insensitive or cruel behavior, hurt or frighten others and on occasion even contribute to their anger. This is not to say we "make people angry" but that we can contribute to their anger.

Caution: If your partner acts out inappropriately with hurt or anger, you are not to be held accountable for that behavior. The important thing is to understand the connection between actions and feelings—both yours and theirs. My actions can have an effect on you, and yours can have an effect on me.

Try this exercise: For several days monitor your reactions to your partner's emotions. Notice if there is any way in which you influenced (not been responsible for) his/her behavior or feelings. Then try for a few days to monitor your own behavior and feelings and notice if your partner contributes in any way. Again, don't hold him/her responsible, but just look for influence.

Try this: Another way to increase your attunement is to notice and tune into your body's reactions to others' emotional or verbal expressions. You can listen and care with your entire body. You may feel a slight ache in your chest/heart area, a hollow feeling in your stomach, or an emergence of tears. Your body can be an important source of information, and paying attention to it can be quite helpful. Be careful that you do not overreact and project your experience onto your partner or the person with whom you are trying to be empathic. You may also need to use your body to calm down if your feelings are too strong and get in the way of being present to your partner.

Empathy can also allow you to avoid seeing your partner as right or wrong. If you are both attempting to be tuned in and empathic, you will not get caught up in disagreeing with each other and trying to "win" arguments.

Try this exercise: The next time the two of you begin to disagree on an issue about which you have argued in the past, stop and truly try to understand your partner's feelings and opinions about this problem. Practice all the techniques outlined previously before you attempt to interject your point of view. Ideally your partner will do the same. This will help you to respect each other's differing opinions or values without feeling threatened. And this requires maturity!

This process is not a one-way street. We have to ask questions and to give honest responses. If you sense sadness, convey your concern with an inquiry not a declaration that you "know what they are feeling." Then your partner can be candid and not just agree with your assessment but report what it is they are feeling. And you may be right after all!

Validate your assumptions about what another person is feeling/ thinking before you congratulate yourself for being "tuned in."

Empathy bridges the gap between two people, but to be effective it requires effort and openness on both parts. On one side it requires listening, asking questions, being receptive, watching closely, and being perceptive. On the other side, it requires candor, honesty, and self-disclosure.

We all have different emotional needs and ways of communicating, but these are the basics for everyone. Take some time right now and write out a brief description or list of your emotional needs. You may even want to keep these posted in a convenient place for easy reference.

My Emotional Needs:
1. I need to have my feelings respected.
2. Please ask me what I am feeling—don't tell me.
3.
4.
5.
6.
7.
8.

I haven't said much about sensitivity in this and other chapters but would be remiss not to mention this perhaps misused and overused concept. In a way, empathy and attunement are simply more accurate terms for what we all call sensitivity. Take a few moments to think and then make a list of the ways in which your partner is sensitive to you, your feelings, and your needs. Do the same for the way you are sensitive to him/her.

Ways My Partner Is Sensitive to Me
1. He/she always asks about my day.
2.
3.
4.
5.

Ways I Am Sensitive to My Partner
1. I listen carefully when he/she is upset about something.
2. I ask appropriate questions.
3.
4.
5.

Does this sensitivity reflect the same ingredients outlined previously for empathy, attunement, and compassion? Does it include careful listening, acknowledging feelings, asking questions, and respecting needs? Some of us declare that we are sensitive people when the reality is that we may be sensitive about and not very sensitive to. Think about the difference. The first is about you; the second is about others. For example, you may get hurt easily, but do you know when you hurt others?

Use these questions and statements on an ongoing basis to help you evaluate your interactions. Keep them available on 3 x 5 cards or post them on your refrigerator.

- "What do you think about _____?" (Sincerely inviting an opinion.)

- "Are you feeling _____?" (Be open for an honest answer or correction.)

- "Will you please tell me what you need?"

- "May I tell you what I hear you saying?"

- "Let me tell you what I'm feeling."

- "I'm truly sorry you had/have to experience _____."

- "I'm sorry, but I wasn't paying attention. Could you please say that again?"

- "Let me ask you a question about that." (A shared thought, feeling, or experience.)

- "I would be interested in hearing about _____."

If you can practice and internalize the exercises suggested in this chapter, you will have mastered perhaps the second most important component of EQ.

* * *

Let's move now to working on an EQ quality that will help you look for the best in yourself and your partner—the silver lining, the upside of things, the possibilities, and the solutions. In Chapter 12, I will show you how to develop/increase an attitude of hope and optimism. If this is already your approach to life and to your relationship, good for you!

CHAPTER TWELVE

A Positive Attitude

Maintaining Hope and Optimism

Life is a shipwreck but we must not
forget to sing in the lifeboats.

—VOLTAIRE

I always plucked a thistle and planted a flower
where I thought a flower would grow.

—ABRAHAM LINCOLN

Would you say that marriage is a relationship that actually works well? Or would you be more likely to say that there are very few happy marriages?

Positive psychologists would argue that to achieve the former requires a hopeful and optimistic attitude and that this possibility exists within all of us. There are happy marriages, and it is possible for you to have one. Having this belief helps relationships/marriages to be successful. There are many reasons for this, so read on.

THE CORNERSTONE

In this segment I am treating a positive attitude as the key emotional intelligence (EQ) quality to work toward, with hopefulness and optimism being subsets of this attitude. This also includes such concepts as faith, trust, and confidence.

Some personality experts claim that a positive or negative outlook is an inborn temperament, a natural trait. Similarly, other researchers label this quality as "dispositional optimism" or "dispositional pessimism," meaning that it is a relatively consistent part of your personality. This implies that it is to some degree a given in who you are. Whether inborn and consistent or not, this EQ quality can also be developed or learned with effort. If you are not naturally a positive, optimistic person, work on it! It will enrich your life. Your inborn temperament is not necessarily your destiny.

As an exercise in self-awareness, look back over your childhood, youth, and adult years and try to recall whether you have always had a more positive outlook or a more negative one. As you have maneuvered the ups and downs of life, has your approach been optimistic and hopeful or pessimistic and negative? Or has your fundamental attitude changed over time? This may help you to determine whether this quality comes naturally to you or not. Also try to recall any times in your life when you had to make a concerted effort to view yourself, life, people, and circumstances in a more positive way.

We all develop what is called an "explanatory style." This has to do with the way we explain the things that happen to us. If you are a pessimist, you are more likely to see bad things as permanent and uncontrollable and good things as just a matter of chance. You are likely to use phrases like "this *always* happens," "you *never* do . . . ," or "things will *never* change."

If you explain good events or successes in permanent and universal terms but bad events or setbacks in temporary and specific terms, this will serve you well.

If you are an optimist, you are likely to see bad things as temporary and controllable and good things as deserved or expected. You might say "this rarely happens," "you fail to do this at times," or "things will get better."

A pessimist gets discouraged and gives up. An optimist has a healthy self-serving and self-protective bias that things will turn out OK. This will be discussed further in the next section on self-efficacy. Suffice it to say, things are mostly as you perceive or interpret them, not as they appear on the surface.

Positivism, hope, and optimism constitute a thread that runs through all EQ. Also, as with all other aspects of EQ, self-awareness is key. You may not always be aware when you are being negative and pessimistic; therefore, once again, examine your level of self-awareness or ways to improve it.

It is important to know that positive and negative emotions are not polar opposites. In other words, it is normal to have both kinds of feelings; however, it is best if the positive is predominant in the way you view yourself, your partner, life in general, and your relationship/marriage. A good resource to help you test or measure this aspect of your EQ is to read and then take the self-tests in *Authentic Happiness* by Martin Seligman, Ph.D.

A PRACTICE EXERCISE

To practice self-awareness for this aspect of EQ, begin by tuning in to your own feelings, perceptions, attitudes, thoughts, words, and behaviors; stop yourself in your tracks to transform those that are negative into positive, those that are hopeless into hopeful, those that are pessimistic into optimistic. Use the following exercise to help you in this process:

Step One: When you first begin to work on this, pay close attention to your feelings, thoughts, attitudes, words, and actions throughout the day. Remember—this is being aware without being self-absorbed!

Step Two: Notice at any point in your day if you are saying negative things, thinking in a pessimistic way, acting out negatively, or feeling hopeless. Completely cease what you are doing.

Step Three: Take three or four deep, cleansing breaths, breathing in through your nose and out through your mouth. This breathing exercise helps you let go of distractions and relax for a few moments.

Step Four: Shift your focus to the negativity you were experiencing and ask yourself three questions: Why am I thinking/feeling/acting this way?

Step Five: Whether you get an answer or not, move on to asking yourself what hopeful, optimistic, or positive options you have with which to replace the negativity.

Step Six: Apply this new thought, feeling, or behavior to the current situation or any that come up in the next few hours.

Step Seven: If you feel it would be helpful, make a brief notation in your journal or on your computer about this experience and date it. This may be useful to you at a later time.

Reminder: Try this exercise for at least a month on a regular basis. Pay close attention to your relationship as you use this process. Apply it primarily to your interactions with your partner.

Over time you will not have to go through this exercise because you will more easily be positive and optimistic in your life and in your relationship. It is a common excuse or argument to claim that you are "just a realist" and are not being negative, that your life situation really is awful, or that your partner is truly irritating and you have a right to complain. Realism and optimism/positivism are not mutually exclusive. These are compatible views or perspectives. You can be both realistic and optimistic at the same time. Life is awful at times, and our partners can be irritating. This is not to suggest "Pollyanna" thinking or denial. An emotionally intelligent person is realistic and still applies optimism to life, putting a positive spin on things as much as possible.

All relationships go through difficulties, and we all act like "jerks" to our partners at one time or another. Believing the best about your partner and yourself will reap benefits far more than looking for the worst.

Try this exercise: For several days pay close attention to the things that usually upset you about your partner. Instead of getting distressed by these issues, think of something positive about your mate on which to focus your attention. You may find it useful to write these down.

Examples are provided to get you started:

Things That Drive Me Mad	Things on Which I Can Focus As Alternatives
1. My partner needs to lose weight.	1. He/she wants to be healthy and active.
2. My partner gets angry too easily.	2. He/she is aware of this and working on it.
3. My partner is always grouchy after work.	3. He/she needs some "down time" after a stressful day.
4.	4.
5.	5.
6.	6.
7.	7.
8.	8.

After you have done this for several days, discuss it with each other. You may have to ask for a change if something inappropriate has been occurring. But you can make this request with empathy and using the other skills you are learning. Or you can share with your partner that you see positive things in him/her and that you are trying to allow these to overshadow the negative. Wouldn't you like to have this done in return? Decide as a couple to use this approach consistently. Your EQ will increase. Do this for a lifetime.

OPTIMISTS OFFER ENCOURAGEMENT

Optimists have smoother and more satisfying relationships than do pessimists. This is partially true because pessimists are more likely to expect the worst and more likely to become depressed when bad things happen.

As you may well know, the things you admired about your partner when you first met may have faded over time. It is important to try to keep admiration alive or to find new traits that you appreciate in each other. This is an area of your relationship in which positive thinking and optimism are needed.

For approximately a month focus only on your partner's good qualities or strengths and not at all on his/her negative qualities or weaknesses. If you have difficulty with this exercise, it might help you to write them down. Make a list of at least ten of his/her pleasing qualities. Keep this list handy for reference.

A process such as this tends to snowball or feed on itself.

If I expect the best of you, I am more likely to receive the best; if I focus on what displeases me about you and expect the worst, I will probably get it.

THOUGHT STOPPING AND THOUGHT DISPUTATION

The current dominant view on the cause and effect relationship between thoughts and feelings is that thoughts lead to emotions. In the past it was seen as being the other way around—that emotion leads to thought. The truth lies somewhere in the middle. For the development of EQ, I lean toward thoughts leading to feelings, but this can and does occur the other way around as well.

You can learn to be more positive by disputing your own thoughts, perceptions, and beliefs. As with other aspects of EQ, you first have to be aware of and recognize your negative thoughts and beliefs to dispute them. This initial step is called thought stopping. You can learn to recognize when you are having a negative or unproductive thought and just "stop yourself in your tracks," and replace it with something else.

A common example in your relationship might be "my wife is no fun any more" or "my husband is always such a jerk." You can train yourself to notice when you are having such thoughts and say instead, "I need to find more fun activities for us to do together because it is not her style to suggest such things" or "I do get so frustrated with my husband, but I need to remember that he can also be . . . (good quality)." This is disputing a thought—not just replacing it.

For the next few weeks keep a record of your reactions to certain events that occur in your life, particularly between you and your partner. Pay close attention to your negative reactions and list them opposite your record of events. Finally, opposite this part of the record write out things that dispute your negativity. These items might include alternative ways of thinking, facts that prove the negative thoughts incorrect, possible solutions to the problems about which you are concerned, and anything else you find useful to dispute your negativity and replace it with something more positive.

You might set up a chart like the one below to help you with this process:

Event	➤ Negative Thought/Belief	➤ Alternative (Positive Thought/Belief)
Your partner doesn't hear something you have said.	"He/she never listens to me."	"He/she has been under a lot stress and is focused on something else at this moment."

This exercise requires some work, but such is the nature of relationships/marriage. It pays off!

Another bad habit common in couples is fostering and hanging on to negative thoughts about ongoing issues or past memories. This is more destructive than negative thoughts about current issues. For example, you may persistently think of your partner as someone who has hurt or mistreated you and will always hurt or mistreat you. If you fail to take appropriate action in responding to what is going on between you and your partner and just continue ruminating about the past issue, these thoughts will become habitual and erode your relationship.

Similarly, if you consistently think of your partner as somehow inferior and yourself as superior, you take the risk of developing toxic thoughts that can become erosive. Things deteriorate in part because you might not even notice those times when he/she is being the ideal partner or making changes you have requested. This poisonous rumination is usually quite powerful. It becomes habit forming and automatic.

Forgiveness is sometimes difficult, but you cannot be married without it. You will be surprised when you begin to track and then reverse these deeper, more toxic patterns. At first you resist letting go because of hurt, anger, and disappointment. But if you can conquer these negative feelings, you will have greater peace of mind (and improved EQ)!

THE INTERACTION BETWEEN YOUR SELF-ESTEEM AND POSITIVE/NEGATIVE THINKING

Optimism and maintaining a positive, hopeful attitude correlate with self-esteem. If you tend to have higher self-esteem, you are more likely to have an optimistic explanatory style regarding what occurs in your life. If your self-esteem tends to be lower, you are more pessimistic and expect negative outcomes for yourself and your future. This carries over into your relationships.

Below is a list of things to consider for achieving or increasing your self-esteem. Use it over time to evaluate your efforts in building or sustaining your own self-esteem. Keep it handy and practice some of these suggestions on a regular basis.

- Refrain from being too hard on yourself—criticizing yourself excessively.

- Be authentic—allow yourself to be who you really are.

- Affirm yourself regularly.

- Be aware of your feelings and express them.

- Don't rely on others to validate you. This should be mostly internal.

- Don't be a people pleaser; be true to yourself.

- Take responsibility for your own behavior, feelings, and life in general.

- Don't be a victim or one who blames others.

- Stay away from critical or judgmental people as much as you can.

- Reframe negative comments made to or about you in such a way as to be useful to you.

- Make a list of your positive qualities or attributes as well as successes, and keep this list handy for quick reference. Add to the list over time.

- Take care of yourself in all areas: physically, emotionally, spiritually, socially, professionally.

- Don't give your power away. Run your own life.

- State your needs and find ways to get them met.

- Laugh at yourself but not in a destructive way.

- Set goals and achieve them, but be realistic—don't set the bar so high that you set yourself up for failure.

THE ROLE OF SPIRITUALITY

This quality of EQ (being positive, hopeful, and optimistic) overlaps significantly with your religious and/or spiritual beliefs. Hope is the aspect of a positive attitude that is most connected to your spiritual life. Having hope is a cornerstone to the teachings of most of the world's major religions and is one aspect of what it means to be spiritually mature. Essentially, if you develop and are mature in your religious or spiritual beliefs and behaviors, this will increase your ability to be hopeful and optimistic.

Optimism and hope are largely about something in the future—whether it is ten minutes or ten years from now. They help us focus on what could be—on what is possible. The familiar reassuring statement, "this too shall pass," is said to have originated with Abraham Lincoln. Despite a depressive disorder, he was determined to be hopeful! And it is our faith and religious or spiritual path that ideally leads to a belief that things will get better, to an attitude of hope.

You can learn to use a self-guided imagery process about future events, interactions with your partner, or challenges you are facing in any aspect of your life.

Try this exercise. It could take 30 minutes or longer.

Step One: Find a quiet comfortable place where you can relax and ideally lay down. At home this could be a sofa, bed, or comfortable spot on the floor. If you are at work, you may just push back, stretch out your feet, and lean back in a chair.

Step Two: Remove all distractions (i.e., turn off your phones, lock your door, etc.).

Step Three: Turn on soft, soothing music if you have it available.

Step Four: Loosen your clothing a bit, close your eyes, relax, and begin to deepen and slow your breathing; breathe in through your nose and out through your mouth three to four times.

Step Five: Continue to breathe slowly and deeply; tighten and then relax each part of your body, beginning with your feet and moving to the top of your head.

Step Six: Imagine that you are at a favorite place such as near a stream, on a mountain top, near the ocean, in your back yard. Visualize yourself there for a couple of minutes.

Step Seven: Allow yourself to focus on a situation or person about which you need to be more positive or hopeful. Visualize things as you would like them to be—as they could be—and imagine your role or attitude as being optimistic and receptive of a positive outcome.

Step Eight: Focus on this situation (and allow yourself to be there) for as long as you would like.

Step Nine: Open your eyes. Resume regular breathing. Get up slowly and move around.

Step Ten: You may want to jot down a few notes about the images that emerged for you and about how things could be.

Step Eleven: Return to your regular activities, trying to maintain this image whenever you encounter the person or situation about which you need to change your view.

This exercise is presented as spiritual because it brings you close to your inner self, core, spirit, or soul. In using this exercise, you may also find it helpful to pray, meditate, or commune with God/Universal Force.

Some religious or spiritual traditions teach that you can affect the outcomes of your life by what you think and believe. These traditions would claim that "you get what you put out there." In other words, if you expect the best and have positive expectations, you will receive the best and experience hoped-for outcomes. In traditional Christian terms this might be similar to a belief that prayers can be answered with a hoped-for outcome.

KEEP A RECORD

Another technique that helps with this aspect of EQ is to record the positive aspects of a situation, relationship, or person, especially your partner. When you find yourself grumbling and being negative or hopeless about something, take time to capture these feelings in a constructive way that reverses or softens the attitudes.

Something that has proven useful to millions is the use of a "gratitude journal." Take a few minutes daily to record or think about the things for which you are grateful or thankful. This may be as few as five items or as many as twenty-five. It can be as simplistic as "I am able to breathe today" to as complex as "I have a wonderful family, job, and lifestyle" or "My wife/husband and I resolved that issue peacefully." This gratitude journal can be a real gift when applied to your relationship. What are you grateful for in your relationship? Record this. Then share it.

If it works for you to record the negatives in your life first and then the positives and this leads to a shift in your thinking or feelings, do it. Be consistent with this daily for several weeks or until it comes naturally for you to have an "attitude of gratitude."

This is another way to reframe things. The root word for gratitude is grace, which means a gift from God.

Recall and record things for which you are grateful from the past that your partner did for you or gave you. Now do the same thing for the present. Be consistent with this, possibly even doing it daily. As often as possible, thank your partner for the things you have recorded. This not only helps you become more emotionally intelligent, but it strengthens the bond of love between you and him/her. One possible outcome is that it might help you forgive your partner for his/her weaknesses or mistakes. And look in a mirror! Face your own mistakes and forgive yourself as well.

HEALTH AND WELLNESS

If you exercise regularly and are well fed, rested, and physically fit, you are more likely to be able to be positive and hopeful.

One final exercise: Find times when you can slow down, relax, and focus or be mindful of the things you really enjoy. Breathe deeply for a minute and allow your mind to go to these pleasant experiences or aspects of your life. This might be a warm bath, the laughter of your children, good food, a long bike ride, or a special time with your partner. You will find that this strengthens your ability to focus on gratitude, promotes a more positive attitude in general, and helps you feel better physically.

The key here is that chronic emotional distress (including negativity and pessimism) is toxic to your body while positive and hopeful attitudes promote physical health, healing, and well-being. There is considerable evidence to support this idea.

Having the ability to be hopeful can be beneficial in a number of areas in your life. If you are a hopeful person, you are more likely to:

- **Maintain better health and wellness.**

- **Persist in finding different ways to reach your goals.**

- **Be self-motivated (discussed in Chapter 15).**

- **Be more resourceful in maneuvering your way through problems.**

- **Be self-reassuring when the going gets tough.**

• • •

Now, if you can maintain this optimistic attitude, you are ready to move forward to the next EQ quality: Self-efficacy. What is this? It is a belief that you are not a victim of circumstance but are instead the "captain of your ship" and that you have some power over how things turn out for you and your partner.

CHAPTER THIRTEEN

Maintaining a Sense of Self-Efficacy

People who believe they have the power to
exercise some measure of control over their lives
are healthier, more effective, and more successful
than those who lack faith in their ability
to effect changes in their lives.

—ALBERT BANDURA, PH.D.

N ow you know that you can change the way you think and that you can even change the way you feel. Have you ever thought that how you interpret things (your belief system) is more powerful than what is actually happening? As a couple, if you and your partner can develop and maintain a sense of self-efficacy, you will feel more successful as a team.

WHAT IS SELF-EFFICACY?

Self-efficacy refers to having a sense or belief that you can impact the outcome of what happens to you. It plays an important role in your ability to use any of your skills to deal with the problems or circumstances you face.

If you believe you can, you can! This component of emotional intelligence (EQ) requires persistence and enthusiasm. You cannot be self-efficacious without persistence and enthusiasm; conversely, these qualities will likely lead to more self-efficacy. It's circular.

This is not about your actual skills but is about your belief or judgment of your ability to affect outcomes and to cope. As a couple, the greater your sense of self-efficacy, persistence, and enthusiasm, the more confidence you will have to meet the challenges that you face together. This can differ from one behavior or situation to another. It becomes more important when things are really difficult. The opposite of having self-efficacy is to feel powerless and to doubt your ability to meet challenges and get through hard times.

For example, I recently spoke with a highly successful and professionally competent man who didn't believe he could meet for dinner with his current partner and one of her former love partners with whom she continued a friendship. While this could clearly be a difficult situation, it was not impossible and had the potential for a positive outcome. He did ultimately attend the dinner and felt more empowered as a result.

PRACTICING SELF-EFFICACY

It is best to begin with those activities and behaviors that are easiest for you, but don't stop with these or you will never strengthen this aspect of your EQ. It's amazing what you can do when you believe you can and put forth the effort. You will be less likely to feel like a victim or to be a quitter.

Try this: Make a list of the things in your relationship about which you feel confident or that give you a strong sense of personal power. Push yourself to list as many of these as possible.

1. I have the ability to listen patiently to my partner.

2. I am comfortable being affectionate with my partner.

3. I can easily express my need for _____.

(Continue to at least 10.)

It is also helpful to look at this list as often as possible and give yourself credit for your successes and the things you can manage or be efficacious about. Affirming yourself and each other for your effort and strengths will help you face those things in which you lack confidence.

Now list those activities or situations between you and your partner that cause you to give up or in which you feel powerless.

1. I can't handle it when we spend all day with his/her family.

2. I can't handle the sexual demands of my partner.

3. I'll never be able to hold my own in a disagreement with him/her.

(Continue to at least 10.)

Again, push yourself to list as many as possible. Identifying the issues you find challenging or anxiety producing is an important step in developing a sense of self-efficacy. It is rooted, like all other aspects of EQ, in self-awareness and self-knowledge.

Now, for each of these issues or circumstances, think about a solution or a way to feel more powerful when you face them. It's easy to focus on problems and not stop to think about solutions, to complain and carry on about what you "can't handle." But the challenge of constructing solutions can make you feel empowered and in control of your life/relationship.

When you are doubting the outcome of a situation, try the:

Stop, breathe, center, think/feel, and *act/speak* exercise. Below is a shortened version of this exercise for use in building your self-efficacy.

1. *Stop* and *focus* on whatever challenge or situation you are up against.

2. *Breathe* so that you can *relax* and be more prepared to face the challenge.

3. Go into your *center* and listen to the voice of wisdom that gives you reassurance or guidance.

4. Get as clear as possible on what you are *thinking* and *feeling*.

5. Construct a plan of action for dealing with the challenge.

6. Imagine yourself succeeding at whatever you attempt. Focus on the details.

7. Repeat this as often as necessary.

YOU CAN CHANGE THE WAY YOU THINK

At times you need to modify your thoughts and shift from hopeless thoughts to determination. You may have to step back and really ponder or do some note taking on just what is appropriate for a tough situation. For example, if you and your partner are having a major disagreement, take the time you need to be totally honest with yourself. Don't rationalize or be in denial to make it easier or more comfortable. Replace thoughts that are not helpful or will only make things worse with thoughts that will help settle your disagreement. Then when you are ready take the actions or speak the words that will produce the best outcome for you.

A universal habit seems to be to focus on problems and not on solutions. Be sure you direct your attention to a solution! This can clear your head and allow you to concentrate on a positive outcome. You can learn to think better under stress once you truly believe in your problem-solving efficacy.

Think of a situation that comes up for the two of you and take a minute to imagine using this process. Later, when appropriate, practice the exercise fully in a specific circumstance. Using thought changing on a regular basis is important to consistently put forth effort. Remember that enthusiasm and persistence are two additional aspects of EQ that form the bedrock of self-efficacy. If you are generally an enthusiastic and persistent person in the face of difficulties, you are likely to already possess the quality of self-efficacy. If not, these components will have to be developed to enhance your interactions with your mate.

Another effective technique is:

1.   Identify people in your life who appear to be self-efficacious in the areas that are difficult for you. Remember that our focus is on EQ in committed love relationships so it might require witnessing the interactions of other individuals who are in such relationships.

2.   Perhaps you can trust and rely on the self-report of these role models or get them to cooperate with you in doing some informal interviews.

3.   Keep a record of all you observe, learn, or gain from these individuals and then emulate this as often as possible.

4.   Keep them informed of your efforts to pattern their attitudes or behaviors.

5.   Ask for their support.

You can work on this alone or as a couple. Having support and encouragement is essential when we are learning new and difficult ways of being, and so you may want to also discuss your efforts with a close friend or therapist. If you are working on this independently and your partner is supportive, share with him/her what you are doing and ask for their encouragement.

GIVE YOURSELF A BOOST

Inventory Your Success

1. Make a list of the situations in which you were able to overcome difficult odds and do something that helped you feel self-efficacious. Some would call this a feeling of personal empowerment.

2. Try to list as many of these successes as possible. They may be major accomplishments such as "I put myself through college" or lesser hurdles such as "I asked someone out on a date who I didn't think would agree to go out with me. They refused and I handled it very well."

3. Next list what it was you did to overcome any fears, self-doubt, desires to give up and quit, and erratic thinking.

4. Focus on situations that relate to your love relationship.

5. Remember that success breeds success!

When I Showed Self-Efficacy	What I Did to Make It Happen
1. I have learned to be comfortable with my in-laws.	1. I made an effort to get to know them better.
2.	2.
3.	3.
4.	4.
5.	5.
6.	6.
7.	7.

Remember, this goes beyond just feeling confident. It involves convincing yourself that you can affect outcomes despite adverse demands or circumstances. You will feel less like a victim. This requires decisiveness. Make a conscious decision that you are going to face whatever changes are required and then expend whatever effort is necessary. Believe that you can *make things happen*, and you will. You cannot change your partner, but you can change the way you interact with him/her.

Imitate the Famous

Another useful tool is to read the biographies of some of the world's greatest and most influential people. These might be political figures, sports heroes, scientists, great artists, philosophers, performers, or renowned authors. If you study the lives and belief systems of these individuals and try to emulate them, you will be pleased with the results. Think of well-known, successful people whom you admire. Read about their life histories and what they did to succeed or what obstacles they had to overcome. Then write out on 3 x 5 cards some of their views and actions that led them to great achievements. Your goal may not be great achievement, but your relationship will certainly benefit from more personal empowerment.

Change Your Self-Talk

The process of changing your self-talk is essential when using the other tools. You can learn this through reading, observing others, therapy, or just stopping to take the time to practice—saying to yourself what it is you need to hear. Consider the following, and keep this listhandy.

- I can hang in there and keep trying.

- This may take a long while, but it will be worth it.

- I've succeeded in creating an outcome similar to this in other situations. I can do it here.

- Facing defeat or setbacks is just a part of life.

- Even though this is frustrating, I have the ability to face it.

- My love relationship is so important that it is worth the effort; I can do this.

- If I take one step at a time, I know I can do this.

Insight may be helpful. You might benefit from reviewing your history. Who or what influenced your beliefs in your own personal power? The degree to which you were encouraged as a child to believe in your ability to succeed and to face obstacles affects how you do this today.

Try Something New

Another useful approach for increasing your self-efficacy is to choose something in which to develop a competency. For example, you could learn to swim, golf, ski, paint, play an instrument, return to school, get a job, or do public speaking. This is likely to increase your confidence and self-esteem as well as create a sense that you have some power in your life. After you achieve one thing move on to another that is equally or more challenging and then on to another and so on. Make a list of possibilities and get suggestions from your partner, a friend, or a therapist. It can be fun to do this together in your relationship.

Examine Your Explanations

Generally speaking, we are not born with specific tendencies to interpret or make sense of what happens to us. These tendencies are learned and can therefore be relearned. We are all familiar with the term *attribute*, which means "to credit to." In other words, we attribute this event to that cause or attribute this outcome to that influence. An example might be "I attribute my headache to the fact that I injured my head," "I attribute the conflict in our relationship to our need to learn better communication skills," or "I attribute my grade of A+ in this class to the fact that I studied very hard."

This is related to the idea of explanatory style, which was discussed earlier. If you use positive explanations and see things as having positive causes, you will feel less defeated by life's setbacks or the difficulties you have as a couple.

You can change habitual ways of interpreting the causes of things that happen just as you can learn to change pessimistic interpretations to more optimistic ones. This can help you to see your partner and the things that occur between you through more "rose-colored" glasses.

Pay attention to how much personal power and optimism you use in this process. Complete this sentence to make yourself more aware of your belief system whenever difficult situations arise in your relationship/marriage:

I attribute _____to_____.
                         (occurrence)   **(cause)**

REVISIT THE VALUE OF PERSISTENCE

Some of us display a dogged persistence and unyielding enthusiasm in tackling any challenge. You, or someone you know, may be naturally gifted with these qualities; they may represent inherent personality traits. If you are not so lucky, remember that your temperament can be adjusted through experience. So if you are not naturally persistent and tend to give up in the face of defeat, you may have to practice the techniques suggested here—over and over again!

Research shows that the more you persist, the more motivated you are and the more you feel like you have mastery over your life and can meet its challenges. Consider these words of wisdom: "The most successful people are those who know how to fail." Essentially if you hang in there or bounce back when you fail, you will feel your self-efficacy. You can learn to look for what will go right and not what will go wrong in your life and in your love relationship.

You will see a constructive relationship between your actions and attitudes and the outcomes in your life and your relationships. You are the captain of your own ship.

"I want what I want when I want it." Sound familiar?

• • •

The EQ quality addressed in Chapter 14 can be a difficult one. You will need to use some of the other skills you have been practicing to help you work on this one. Our "small child in a grown-up body" doesn't always want to postpone getting what he/she wants or refrain from acting out. But if your goal is a relationship that runs smoothly, delaying gratification and resisting your impulses is a must.

CHAPTER FOURTEEN

Delaying Gratification and Resisting Impulses

Delaying gratification is a process of scheduling
the pain and pleasure of life in such a way as
to enhance the pleasure by meeting and
experiencing the pain . . . .

—M. Scott Peck, M.D., in *The Road Less Traveled*

WHAT IS GRATIFICATION?

There are different ways to view the concept of gratification. In *Authentic Happiness*, Seligman focuses on the gratification that comes from having a sense of accomplishment for a job well done and of being totally immersed in something meaningful and challenging that utilizes your best skills and requires you to be totally focused. Think about it. Haven't we all said, "I get such gratification from _____ (gardening, teaching, painting, carpentry, my work)."

Gratification can also be looked at as pleasure seeking. In other words, we all seek certain pleasures to make us feel gratified—food, drink, television, sex, gambling, spending money, projecting our anger on others. As an aspect of emotional intelligence (EQ), the delay of gratification is linked to resisting your impulses. Having the ability to delay, postpone, or resist such gratifications or impulses as those listed above is clearly a sign of maturity and reflective of having strong EQ. The opposite of this is "I want what I want when I want it" or "I'll do or say whatever and whenever I please." Obviously, this doesn't work in a committed relationship.

There is some evidence that your ability to delay gratification is a given, fixed trait—something with which you are born. The same is true for your level of impulsivity. Whether they are inborn or learned, these are qualities you can identify in yourself; and they can be changed.

If you can delay gratifying your needs when necessary and can resist following your impulses, you are likely to be fundamentally conscientious, self-disciplined, and dependable. And think about how valuable these qualities are to your partner. You already have EQ in this area. Lack of these qualities can lead to some bad habits. But don't despair, you can get rid of such habits.

YOUR PERSONAL HISTORY

This aspect of EQ is clearly related to your upbringing and early life experience. You can begin to work on this by asking yourself questions about your early life such as:

- Was I required to wait for the things I wanted?

- Did I have to earn my rewards?

- Was I held accountable for my actions?

- Was I given limits and required to live by rules and boundaries?

- Was I given adequate responsibilities?

- Did my parents or caregivers always give in to my demands or desires?

- Was I seen as a demanding and impatient child/teen? Was I a bully?

- Did my caregivers use appropriate discipline with me?

The ineffective handling of any of these can result in you having a great deal of difficulty in delaying gratification or resisting impulses as an adult.

Additional influences are your parents, siblings, and others. Try to recall if your parents delayed their gratification and controlled their impulses.

- Were they demanding with you and/or others?

- Did they hold others accountable but not themselves?

- Did they insist on having things their way despite the needs and feelings of others?

- Were they impatient and expected others to do things immediately?

- Did they always selfishly meet their own needs and disregard those of others?

Goleman claims that resisting impulses is the most fundamental of all psychological skills and the root of all emotional self-control—a very strong statement. If you learned to resist impulses and temptations as a small child, you are likely to cope more effectively with life's frustrations, and a relationship/marriage certainly does provide us with frustration.

WHERE ARE YOU NOW?

You can evaluate yourself on your current level of delaying gratification and impulse control.

- Do you get very upset when facing a stressful situation? At work? In your relationship?

- Can you remain focused and calm when under pressure? At work? In your relationship?

- Do you persist or tend to give up in the face of obstacles? At work? In your relationship?

- Are you self-reliant in solving problems, or do you rely on others for problem solving?

- Do you love challenges or shrink from them?

- Do you set goals and work towards them by delaying desires that might interfere?

- Can you wait patiently for the material things you want?

- Do you make demands of your partner just to gratify yourself?

- Are you patient with your partner in getting your needs met?

Even though you may not be a person who naturally likes to delay getting what you want and to control your impulses, you can—through your own efforts and the help of others—learn to be comfortable with doing so. Some would claim that having these abilities shows your level of moral development and character. There may be some truth to this because they depend so much on your temperance and self-control.

It will help you to work on this by considering the questions below. Also ask your partner how they would answer these questions as they apply to you.

- Are you self-disciplined—do you do what needs to be done even if you don't want to?

- Do you express your appetites, wants, or desires in an appropriate or moderate way?

- Are you demanding?

- Do you act upon satisfying your needs in a way that does not harm yourself or deprive others, such as your partner?

- Do you keep your impulses in check and resist acting on them until the time is right or not at all?

- Are you able to wait for the things you want without becoming agitated, angry, or anxious?

- Can you control your urges and passions—both emotionally and in your behaviors?

PRACTICE EXERCISES

If you are not a patient person, you will want to focus some time and energy on developing this virtue because patience is intimately tied to the delay of gratification and the resisting of impulses. Make a list of the things about which you are most impatient in your life in general, e.g., being stuck in traffic, waiting in line at a grocery story or theater, hearing noisy children, waiting to be served in a restaurant, listening to someone who speaks very slowly, dealing with an annoying habit of your partner, not getting what you want.

Make it a point for several weeks to put yourself in these situations or be certain to notice when you are. Then practice the *stop, breathe, center, think/feel*, and *act/speak* technique. For example, when you find yourself tempted to be demanding or impatient, to somehow be gratified, try the following steps:

1. Stop whatever you are doing.

2. Take three deep breaths.

3. Relax and get centered.

4. Focus on what it is about which you are feeling impatient.

5. Think about an alternative way to both think and feel about your frustration.

6. Speak or act in a way that reflects more maturity and EQ.

7. Notice how you feel and compare this with how you felt in situations like this before when you demanded immediate gratification or acted out your impulses.

This exercise will not automatically make you a more patient person, but it will teach you that you do have the capacity to be patient if you try. Learning to be patient is guaranteed to contribute in a positive way to your love relationship. There are many situations with our partners that require us to put off getting exactly what we want and doing or saying whatever our impulses dictate.

Emotional intelligence involves using self-control, but this should not be perceived as suppression. Resisting impulses may involve some self-denial and concern for the needs of your partner, but you don't have to suppress your desires completely. This is just a matter of waiting for the opportune time or situation to express them.

As is true with the development of other EQ qualities, it might be helpful to identify a handful of people you know who appear to do a good job of delaying their gratifications and impulses. Observe them and interview them in detail. Ask them how far back this behavior goes—when and how they learned to be this way. Ask them how they maintain this discipline and how it has benefited them. Use these individuals as role models and emulate their behaviors and attitudes.

Sometimes it is wise to observe and study someone who is just the opposite—someone who appears to have no ability to delay his/her gratification or control his/her impulses. Study them as you might study the person who is strong in managing their desires and impulses. Perhaps getting to understand the history, thoughts, feelings, and behaviors of this type of person can help you understand yourself and boost your determination to be the opposite.

DELAYING GRATIFICATION IN YOUR RELATIONSHIP

As you may have experienced, insistence upon immediate gratification and unbridled impulses can create real havoc. Earlier I asked you to list those things about which you are impatient in your life and to plan to work on these over a period of several weeks. Now examine your love relationship in the same way.

- ○ **Do I insist on getting my way with my partner? Am I demanding?**

- ○ **How do I handle that my mate does not always want to have sex when I do?**

- ○ **Do I express other desires appropriately in my marriage?**

- ○ **How often do I set my needs aside in deference to those of my partner?**

- ○ **Do I act impulsively in my relationship?**

- ○ **Do I say whatever I feel like saying to my partner without concern for the outcome?**

- ○ **Do I spend money any way I like without consulting my partner?**

- ○ **Do I wait for things I want without agitation?**

Your partner can be a valuable asset in helping you deal with the issue of gratification and impulse control. Ask him/her to share with you the issues that they feel you need to address. Then ask them to remind you when you are out of control. Appropriate feedback can be remarkably helpful in learning to redirect your desires. Keep this in strict confidence between you and your partner.

This exercise should be done over a period of several months to be effective. If you have a sincere desire to get these areas of your life under control, be open and nondefensive. Your partner may tell you that they see you as eating or drinking too much. This is a touchy issue. Or they may feel that your spending habits appear to be out of control. Another touchy issue. Like all others, this is an area in EQ in which self-awareness is essential!

If you are inclined to overeat, overspend, drink too much, watch too much TV, demand too much sex, or have other unbridled tendencies, you may benefit from a support group or a twelve-step program. Delaying gratification or controlling impulses is much more difficult if you have habits that feel as though they are out of your control. If you are alcoholic or drug addicted or suffer from other addictive disorders, you will most likely need such support and possibly focused treatment. It is much more difficult to develop these EQ abilities if serious addictions go untreated.

One key to impulse control is being able to differentiate between your feelings and your actions or words. Once you are self-aware and can identify your feelings, you can learn to stop yourself midflight and curb your impulse to say or do something to your partner that you might regret. Practice thinking of alternative comments or actions so you don't feel like you are "left hanging" in your interactions.

Try this exercise:

1. Carefully recall or observe several difficult or less than pleasant interactions or incidents between you and your partner.

2. At first it will be most helpful if you choose something that recurs between you, an issue that you cannot seem to resolve.

3. Take notes on what happened and put every effort into being totally objective and self-honest.

4. Step back and determine if you were just trying to gratify your own desires in this incident and/or whether you allowed your verbal or behavioral impulses to run wild.

5. Discuss this with your partner. Get his/her feedback.

Interaction or Incident	What Happens	Cause of Behavior or Verbal Interchange	A Solution
1. We fight over not having sex often enough.	I withdraw and my mate gets angry.	My partner is thinking of his/her needs, not mine.	We need to take time to discuss this, hear each other's viewpoints, and come to a workable solution.
2.			
3.			
4.			
5.			

Eventually you will be able to circumvent self-gratifying and rampant impulses from taking over in stressful situations.

•   •   •

Chapter 15 (the final chapter) could have been the first because being self-motivation takes you full circle through all the fundamentals of taking on the challenge of improving your relationship.

CHAPTER FIFTEEN

Self-Motivation

Look at a day when you are supremely satisfied
at the end. It's not a day when you lounge
around doing nothing, it's when you've had
everything to do and you've done it!

—MARGARET THATCHER

Twenty years from now you will be more
disappointed by the things that you didn't do than
by the ones you did do. So throw off the bowlines.
Sail away from the safe harbor. Catch the trade
winds in your sails. Explore. Dream. Discover.

—MARK TWAIN

In a technical sense, motivation refers to the arousal or initiation, direction, intensity, and persistence of behavior or expenditure of effort. The root Latin origin of motivation is *movere* or "to move." (Ironically, it is also claimed that this is the root word for emotion.) Motivation is one concept that has been studied since antiquity, since the time of Plato and Aristotle. Most current studies of motivation are related to work or academic settings. There are very few that concern the effect of motivation, self-motivation, or the lack thereof in personal relationships.

For our purposes, let's say motivation is effortful, directed action. However, we are focused on the self as the key factor here. Self-motivation is reflected in you taking the initiative, setting the direction, determining the intensity, and persisting in the effort, action, or behavior with which you are faced.

Self-motivation as applied to emotional intelligence (EQ) requires you to be able to manage your thoughts, emotions, and actions in order to put out the necessary effort to reach a goal, accomplish a task, or make a change.

The most dramatic examples of highly self-motivated people are well-known athletes, artists, musicians, writers, and others who face rigorous, persistent training or practice routines and regimens. Use these people as role models, as you have for other EQ qualities.

SELF-MOTIVATION IN YOUR RELATIONSHIP

You may be able to easily see how self-motivation applies to your work or special interests and hobbies, but can you think of ways in which it applies to your relationship/marriage? There are numerous situations in love relationships when this quality of EQ is an absolute necessity! Perhaps thinking of the opposite would be helpful.

Lack of self-motivation can show up as:

○ Your needing to be reminded or pushed to do things

○ The necessity for outside rewards in order for you to take action or make changes

○ A lack of confidence requiring you to depend on the constant support or encouragement of partners

○ A simple unwillingness to put forth the effort required to make important changes

○ Being so image conscious that you will only take action to impress others

○ Using or making excuses for lack of follow through

Your relationship brings with it a lot of responsibility. While it may be less essential than other qualities, self-motivation is definitely a component of EQ that you and your partner need. There are numerous situations which call for this ability; a key example is having a general desire and willingness to work on the relationship itself.

You might be highly motivated in your work or leisure activities but have little motivation to put serious effort into your relationship. Effort for your relationship could require you to read, take inventories, practice relationship-building skills, go on dates, attend couples workshops, or even attend couple therapy.

Much to the dismay of a partner, it is not uncommon for one individual to fail to follow through. Can you relate to this? Do you or your partner put off important things with the excuse of "I was going to get around to it eventually" or "our relationship is just fine the way it is" (when in reality it needs work). It takes self-discipline to face head-on such uncomfortable but immensely important efforts.

Other examples of situations that require self-discipline in your relationship/marriage are listed below. Add to this list and keep it handy to evaluate how you or your partner react to the normal demands of life:

• Dealing with household chores or duties.

• Having financial responsibilities or being a breadwinner.

• Participating in activities together for companionship.

- Facing your parenting responsibilities.

- Practicing and using good communication skills.

- Practicing and using good conflict management skills.

- Being persistent in physical exercise.

- Others?

INTRINSIC VS. EXTRINSIC MOTIVATION

One potentially sticky issue in your relationship may be how to handle intrinsic vs. extrinsic motivation. Intrinsic motivation refers to doing what you do because you enjoy or want to do it for its own sake, for the satisfaction it provides, or because you know it is your responsibility to follow through. This requires no outside rewards or punishments of any kind. It is the most effective type of motivation. Extrinsic motivation is that which requires a push or pull from outside. It is less self-directed and more other directed. Examples in the workplace might be a promotion/demotion or a raise/cut in pay; in an academic setting, a good/bad grade or lots of praise/ridicule; in your relationship, it might be warm expressions of gratitude or a threat of some kind.

So if you are an intrinsically motivated person, you are more self-determining and likely to make a better marital partner. If you are extrinsically motivated, you may be dependent upon your partner to "get you moving" or praise or compliment you or you may rely on other outside rewards or punishments. This can create a drain on your relationship.

Any type of motivation is learned and can be either reinforced and strengthened or unlearned. You are likely to have developed your level of self-motivation or lack thereof as a child due to the atmosphere in your home—either promoting or discouraging.

To assess this, consider the questions below. As you think about these questions, keep in mind that self-motivation can be stifled by too much praise and too many rewards as well as too much punishment or discounting. Yes, your motivation can be lessened if it is too dependent on outside influences, even praise and rewards. You are more likely to have positive outcomes in anything you do if you are self-determining and not influenced too much by outside forces.

○ Were you given responsibilities just as a matter of course as a member of the family? Or were you paid for doing anything to help or punished if you didn't help?

○ Did you do your homework regularly and adequately on your own initiative? Or did your parents/caretakers nag, remind, push, or punish you if you didn't do your homework in a timely, self-initiated fashion?

○ Did you experience, on your own, pleasure and satisfaction for a job well done? Or did you rely on praise and rewards for your accomplishments?

○ Do you recall achievements and accomplishments done entirely for your own sense of satisfaction without any outside rewards or punishments?

○ As you look back, did you see your parents as self-motivated and self-initiating? Or were your parents overly reliant on outside pressure or rewards to fulfill their goals and responsibilities?

○ Were you given the opportunity to help make decisions that affected your life? Or did your parents make all your decisions and essentially tell you what to do?

○ Were you taught not to do certain things simply because they were wrong and might possibly hurt other people? Or do you recall being taught not to do certain things that were wrong because you could be caught and punished?

○ Do you recall being more motivated by a desire to succeed or by a fear of failure?

○ Do you remember doing things to challenge yourself? Or do you recall needing to be challenged by outside forces, either positive or negative?

AUTONOMY

Having the appropriate level of autonomy contributes to the development of your self-motivation. If you and your partner support each other's autonomy, you are more likely to be self-motivated or to develop greater self-motivation.

Rewards can interfere with autonomy as much as overcontrol. You can become overly dependent upon rewards, i.e., the more rewards you get for successes, the more you seem to need them to succeed. Punishments might control you with force, but rewards can control you with seduction. Creating an autonomy-supportive environment offers many benefits.

Or maybe you just naturally want to meet your challenges head on, master lots of skills, and attain competence for the pleasure it gives you. You don't need to be constantly rewarded (extrinsically)! You can reward yourself (intrinsically)!

If you are seriously lacking self-motivation, you may need to acquire the services of a professional or participate in some form of intense retraining.

• • •

It's up to you. You can make the EQ exercises your magic wand—a combination of several can yield remarkable results.

You are the proud owner of increased EQ and a better love relationship. That is if you used this book as your own "personal trainer" and practiced getting your EQ in shape. Congratulations!

FOOTNOTES

••

1. P. Salovey and J.D. Mayer, "Emotional Intelligence," *Imagination, Cognition, and Personality* (Amityville, N.Y.: Baywood Publishing Company, 1990), pp. 185-211.
2. J. Ciarrochi, J.P. Forgas, and J.D. Mayer, Eds., *Emotional Intelligence in Everyday Life* (New York: Psychology Press, 2006).
3. D. Goleman, *Emotional Intelligence* (New York: Bantam Books, 1997).
4. Ibid.
5. M. Matoon, *Jungian Psychology in Perspective* (New York: Simon & Schuster, 1990).
6. S. Johnson, The Practice of Emotionally Focused Marital Therapy: Creating Connection (New York: Brunner/Mazel, 1996).
7. F. Pittman, *Grow Up! How Taking Responsibility Can Make You a Happy Adult* (New York: St. Martin's Press, 1999).
8. D. Goleman, op cit.
9. Ibid.
10. E. Fromm, *The Art of Loving* (New York: HarperCollins, 2000).
11. H. Hendrix, *Getting the Love You Want: A Guide for Couples* (New York: Henry Holt, 2001).
12. F. Pittman, op cit.
13. M. Scott Peck, *The Road Less Traveled (25th Anniversary Edition)* (New York: Simon & Schuster, 2002)
14. L. Buscaglia, *Love: What Life Is All About* (New York: Random House, 1996).
15. J. Gottman, *The Seven Principles for Making Marriage Work* (New York: Crown, 1999).
16. M. Williamson, *A Return to Love: Reflections on the Principles of a Course in Miracles* (New York: HarperCollins, 1996).
17. S. Johnson, op cit.
18. F. Pittman, op cit.
19. Ibid.
20. D. Goleman, op cit.
21. P. Coleman, *How to Say It for Couples: Communicating with tenderness, Openness, and Honesty* (Paramus, N.J.: Prentice Hall Press, 2002).
22. R. Bednar, M. Wells, and S. Peterson, *Self-Esteem: Paradoxes and Innovations in Clinical Theory and Practice* (Washington, D.C.: American Psychological Association, 1993).

23. Ibid.
24. G. Null, *Power Aging* (New York: New American Library, Penguin Group, 2003).
25. S. Keen, *Hymns to an Unknown God: Awakening the Spirit in Everyday Life* (New York: Bantam Doubleday Dell, 1995).
26. M. Sinetar, *A Way Without Words: A Guide for Spiritually Emerging Adults* (New York: Paulist Press, 1992).
27. J. Segal, *Raising Your Emotional Intelligence: A Practical Guide* (New York: Owl Books, 1997).

BIBLIOGRAPHY

Bandura, A. *Self Efficacy: the Exercise of Control.* New York: W. H. Freeman, 1997.

Beattie, M. *Beyond Codependency: And Getting Better all the Time.* San Francisco: Harper and Row, 1999.

Bednar, R., M. Wells, and S. Peterson. *Self-Esteem: Paradoxes and Innovations in Clinical Theory and Practice.* Washington, D.C: American Psychological Association, 1996.

Bernard, J. S., and J. Bernard. *The Future of Marriage.* New Haven: Yale University Press, 1982.

Bowlby, J. *Attachment and Loss. Volume 1: Attachment.* New York: Basic Books, 1969.

Bradshaw, J. *Bradshaw On: the Family.* Deerfield Beach, Fla.: Health Communications, 1990.

Bradshaw, J. *Homecoming: Reclaiming and Championing Your Inner Child.* New York: Bantam Doubleday Dell, 1992.

Branden, N. *Six Pillars of Self-esteem.* New York: Bantam Books, 1995.

Burger, J. M. *Personality.* California: Wadsworth/Thomson Learning, 2000.

Buscaglia, L. *Love: What Life Is All About.* New York: Random House, 1996.

Chapman, G. D., G. Chapman, and J. Bell. *Five Love Languages: How to Express Heartfelt Commitment to Your Mate.* Chicago: Northfield, 1996.

Ciarrochi, J., Forgas, J.P., and Mayer, J.D., Eds. *Emotional Intelligence in Everyday Life.* New York: Psychology Press, 2006.

Coleman, P. W. and P. Coleman. *How to Say it for Couples: Communicating With Tenderness, Openness, and Honesty.* Paramus, N.J.: Prentice Hall Press, 2002.

Cousins, N. *Anatomy of an Illness.* New York: Bantam Books, 1981.

————. *Healing Heart.* New York: Morrow, William, 1984.

Csikszentmihalyi, M. *Flow: the Psychology of Optimal Experience.* New York: HarperCollins, 1991.

DeMaria, R. and M.T. Hannah, Eds. *Building Intimate Relationships: Bridging Treatment, Education and Enrichment Through the PAIRS Program.* New York: Brunner-Routledge. 2003.

Fisher, B. and R. Alberti. *Rebuilding: When Your Relationship Ends.* Atascadero, Calif.: Impact, 1999.

Fowler, J. *Stages of Faith: the Psychology of Human Development.* San Francisco: HarperCollins, 1995.

Fromm, E. *The Art of Loving.* New York: HarperCollins, 2000.

Goleman, D. *Emotional Intelligence.* New York: Bantam Books, 1997.

Gottman, J. and N. Silver. *Why Marriages Succeed or Fail.* New York: Simon and Schuster, 1994.

————. *The Seven Principles for Making Marriage Work.* New York: Crown, 1999

J. Gray. *Mars and Venus in the Bedroom: A Guide to Lasting Romance and Passion.* New York: HarperCollins, 2001.

Griffith, J. and M. Griffith. *The Body Speaks.* New York: Perseus, 1994.

Heitler, S. *The Power of Two.* Oakland, Calif.: New Harbinger, 1997.

Hendrix, H. *Keeping the Love You Find.* New York: Simon & Schuster, 1993.

————. *Getting the Love You Want: a Guide for Couples.* New York: Henry Holt, 2001.

Hopcke, R.H. *A Guided Tour of the Collected Works of C.G. Jung.* Boston: Shambhala, 1992.

James, W. *The Varieties of Religious Experience.* Mineola, N.Y.: Dover, 2002.

Johnson, S. *The Practice of Emotionally Focused Marital Therapy: Creating Connection.* New York: Brunner/Mazel, 1996.

————. *Emotionally Focused Couple Therapy With Trauma Survivors: Strengthening Attachment Bonds.* New York: Guilford, 2002.

Jourard, S. *The Transparent Self.* New York: Van Nostrand Reinhold, 1971.

Jung, J. *The Portable Jung.* New York: Penguin, 1976.

Jung, C. *The Archetypes & the Collective Unconscious (the Collected Works of C. G. Jung), vol. 9.* Princton, N.J.: Princeton University Press, 1980.

Keen, S. *Hymns to an Unknown God: Awakening the Spirit in Everyday Life.* New York: Bantam Doubleday Dell, 1995.

Matoon, M. *Jungian Psychology in Perspective.* New York: Simon & Schuster, 1990.

McGinnis, A. *The Friendship Factor: How to Get Closer to the People You Care For.* Minneapolis, Minn.: Augsburg Fortress, 2004.

Nichols, M. *The Lost Art of Listening.* New York: Guilford, 1996.

Peck, M. Scott. *The Road Less Traveled (25th Anniversary Edition).* New York: Simon & Schuster, 2002.

Pert, C. B. *Molecules of Emotion: The Science Behind Mind-Body Medicine.* New York: Scribner, 2003.

Pittman, F. *Grow Up! How Taking Responsibility Can Make You a Happy Adult.* New York: St. Martin's Press, 1999.

Powell, J. *Happiness is an Inside Job.* Allen, Tex.: More, Thomas, 1997.

Reeve, J. *Understanding Motivation and Emotion.* Princeton, N.J.: John Wiley & Sons, 2002.

Rossi, E. *The Psychobiology of Mind-body Healing.* New York: W.W. Norton, 1993.

Ruiz, M. *The Mastery of Love: a Practical Guide to the Art of Relationship.* San Rafael, Calif.: Amber-Allen, 1999.

Satir, V. *Peoplemaking.* Palo Alto, Calif.: Science & Behavior Books, 1988.

Salovey, P., and J.D. Mayer. "Emotional Intelligence," *Imagination, Cognition, and Personality.* Amityville, N.Y.: Baywood Publishing Company, 1990.

Segal, J. *Raising Your Emotional Intelligence: A Practical Guide.* New York: Owl Books, 1997.

Seligman, M.E.P. *Authentic Happiness: Using the New Positive Psychology to Realize Your Potential for Lasting Fulfillment.* New York: Free Press, 2002.

Siegel, B. *Love, Medicine, and Miracles.* New York: HarperCollins, 1988.

Siegel, D. *The Developing Mind: How Relationships and the Brain Interact to Shape Who We Are.* New York: Guilford, 2002.

Silberman, M. *PeopleSmart: Developing Your Interpersonal Intelligence.* San Francisco: Berrett-Koehler Publishers, 2000.

Sinetar, M. *A Way Without Words: A Guide for Spiritually Emerging Adults.* New York: Paulist Press, 1992.

Steiner, C. *Emotional Literacy: Intelligence with a Heart.* Fawnskin, Calif.: Personhood Press, 2003.

Stern, D. *The Interpersonal World of the Infant: a View from Psychoanalysis and Developmental Psychology.* New York: Basic Books, 2000.

Tannen, D. *You Just Don't Understand: Women and Men in Conversation.* New York: HarperCollins, 2001.

Thorndike, E. *The Psychology of Learning.* New York: Teachers College, Columbia University, 1926.

Thorndike, E. *Human Learning.* New York, London: MIT Press, 1966.

Whitfield, C. *Healing the Child Within.* Pompano Beach, Fla.: Health Communications, 1987.

Williamson, M. *A Return to Love: Reflections on the Principles of a Course in Miracles.* New York: HarperCollins, 1996.

Personality Theories

There are divergent theories of how personality is formed, all of which make contributions to our understanding. Most common among them are psychoanalytical, trait, biological/physiological, humanistic, behavioral/social learning, cognitive, neo-Freudian, and systems theory.

Psychoanalytical argues that our unconscious minds are largely responsible for our behaviors and overall way of functioning in life. (It is important to note that other schools of thought acknowledge the influence of the unconscious as well.)

Trait theory is based on the idea that our personalities are comprised of a set of specific enduring and wide-ranging predispositions. The focus is on the identification and measurement of these various traits.

Biological/physiological explains who we are and how we behave on the basis of inherited predispositions and physiological processes.

Humanistic claims that our behavior and personality are determined by our self-concept and level of self-acceptance. It addresses our choices about how we use our personal responsibility.

Behavioral/social learning claims that we function as we do based on the result of conditioning and expectations, particularly in our youth, although this process continues to some degree throughout our adult years.

Cognitive claims that we are who we are and function as we do based on how we process information; this theory often overlaps with that of the behaviorist.

Neo-Freudian expands the Freudian viewpoint with the belief that we are also influenced by social and cultural forces and with the more optimistic view that we continue to develop throughout our lives.

Systems theory, as used in the field of marriage and family therapy, refers generally to the notion that we are who we are due to the influences of the family system in which we are reared and the one in which we currently find ourselves.

Test Yourself

The following questions will help you assess your level of self-esteem as it relates to your love relationship and your emotional intelligence.

Answer these questions as honestly as you can. Please read each question carefully, as they are all different but may appear to be similar. Do not be distracted if certain questions appear to be assessing the same thing as others.

After you assess yourself, ask your partner to answer the questions as they relate to you. This can contribute to your attunement to him/her.

Use the following scale in answering these questions:

(This is very true for me.) 5 . . . . . 4 . . . . . 3 . . . . . 2 . . . . . 1 . . . . . 0 (This is not at all true for me.)

1. I have a clear understanding of why a person cannot love their partner/spouse if they don't love themselves. _____

2. I have no idea what my level of self-esteem is. _____

3. I am a successful person. _____

4. I don't love myself very much at all. _____

5. I know when my partner is lacking confidence or feeling badly about him/herself. _____

6. I bring neediness and insecurity into my relationship/marriage. _____

7. My level of self-confidence is very high. _____

8. I feel inferior to most other people. _____

9. I believe I have an effect on the outcomes of various aspects of my life. _____

10. I am jealous and possessive in my relationship/marriage. _____

11. I have a positive self-image. _____

12. I am critical or judgmental of other people. _____

13. I understand how I came to have the level of self-esteem that I do. _____

14. It upsets me when I do not please others. _____

15. I am an autonomous person. _____

16. It upsets me when I do not please my partner/spouse. _____

17. I choose to be alone and do activities by myself without my partner/spouse. _____

18. I feel threatened if my partner/spouse chooses to be alone or do activities by him/herself. _____

19. I view my life and its possible outcomes with a positive and hopeful attitude. _____

20. I need quite a lot of positive feedback or reassurances from my partner/spouse. _____

21. I can graciously accept compliments and positive feedback from my partner/spouse. _____

22. I feel threatened when my partner/spouse succeeds at something and feels very good about herself/himself. _____

23. I am able to admit to my partner/spouse the errors or mistakes I make in our relationship. _____

24. I compare myself to my partner/spouse. _____

25. I can "hang in there" and persist in reaching my goals despite obstacles. _____

26. I feel threatened when my partner/spouse strongly disagrees with me. _____

27. I feel badly when my partner is feeling defeated or low. _____

28. I tend to blame my partner/spouse when things go wrong in our relationship. _____

29. I have a hopeful, optimistic attitude about the future. _____

30. I feel superior to a lot of people. _____

The scoring process for this self-esteem inventory is as follows:

Total Your Answers to the Odd Questions

0–25 Low
26–50 Average
51–75 High

Total Your Answers to the Even Questions

51–75 Low
26–50 Average
0–25 High

Religion and Spirituality

Throughout the centuries theologians, great thinkers, and writers have contributed a wealth of wisdom and information on religion and spirituality. What follows is a summary of the thoughts of several renowned contributors who provide a framework that helps us to see the interface between spiritual or religious maturity and emotional intelligence.

Erich Fromm, Ph.D.

- Famed German psychoanalyst; U.S. professor in the mid-twentieth century.

- Classic works: *The Art of Loving, Escape From Freedom, Man For Himself,* and *The Sane Society.*

- Describes the religiously mature person as one who:

    o Is free from the childhood dreams of God as a puppeteer, controlling every aspect of life.

    o Maintains humility and an awareness that we cannot really know the actual nature of God and therefore cannot judge other religions.

- ○ Loves others as much as the self.

- ○ Emphasizes productivity and developing potentialities.

Carl Jung, M.D.

- Swiss psychiatrist; prolific writer and teacher throughout the world (1920s to 1960s).

- Written works are still used worldwide.

- Jungian perspective on religious maturity holds that one must:

  - ○ Become aware of the unconscious religious factors in their psyche.

  - ○ Be aware of his/her inner life and not overly dependent upon creeds and external ethical standards.

  - ○ Avoid conforming to many of the ordinary social expectations of religiosity.

William James, M.D.

- Philosopher and psychologist; taught at Harvard in late 1800s.

- Major contributor to the fields of philosophy and psychology, including *The Principles of Psychology*.

- Described religious maturity as:

  - ○ Having an awareness of being part of a wider world and not being caught up exclusively in this world's selfish little interests.

  - ○ Shifting the emotional center of your life toward loving and harmonious affections with others.

  - ○ Having a conviction of the existence of an "ideal power." (God) with whom you maintain a "friendly continuity."

M Scott Peck, M.D.

- Renowned American author, speaker, and psychiatrist who integrated spiritual and psychological principals and insights.

- Authored *The Road Less Traveled,* which outsold all other books in the United States and around the world than any other at the time (late 1970s).

- Authored best sellers *The People of the Lie* and *A Different Drummer.*

- His theory on spiritual development and spiritual maturity includes:

  o Self-awareness and ownership of one's own destructive behavior as opposed to blaming and projecting onto others.

  o Letting go of dependence upon institutions for a feeling of security and stability.

  o Allowing oneself to go through a period of skepticism in his/her faith and become a "truth seeker."

  o Having a respect for the mystery of God and life and an awareness of how little we know and how much more there is to learn.

  o Maintaining a love of all people.

  o Having an acceptance of values and viewpoints that are different from one's own.

Bernie Siegel, M.D.

- Well-known American physician; left his medical practice to write and speak on the connection between spirituality and healing.

- Popular books include *Love, Medicine and Miracles*; *Your Body Believes Every Word You Say*; *Peace, Love and Healing*; and *Language of Miracles.*

- Says that the spiritual life has many aspects:

  o Self-awareness and ownership of one's own destructive behavior as opposed to blaming and projecting onto others.

  o More than simple piety or a commitment to a religious body.

- A belief in some meaning or order in the universe, seen as God for many.

- A source of healing and a way to find peace.

- The capacity to accept what is and to resolve the contradictions between emotions and reality.

- Teachings in unselfish love including loving enemies as taught by Jesus.

- An open door to finding happiness in an imperfect world and to accepting the self as imperfect.

- Siegel sees God as an intelligent, loving energy and potential healing resource in our lives. He was impressed by the faith of sick and/or dying patients as well as those such as survivors of the Nazi holocaust. I include a quote he frequently referenced which was scratched on a prison wall:

I believe in the sun—even when it does not shine.

I believe in love—even when it is not shown.

I believe in God—even when he does not speak.

The Dalai Lama

- World-renowned Tibetan Buddhist spiritual leader, teacher, and lecturer.

- Nobel Peace Prize winner (1989).

- Teachings about spirituality and religion include:

  - Associating with a particular religion is not in itself a precondition for happiness or ethical conduct.

  - The qualities of love, compassion, patience, tolerance, forgiveness, and humility are essentially spiritual qualities that can be developed in the context of religion if properly employed.

  - All major religions and spiritual paths of the world, despite their differences, are concerned with helping individuals.

become good human beings who have those spiritual qualities.

o   If an individual has developed a firm, grounded faith and it is rooted in some form of daily practice, they generally cope much better with adversity than those who have not.

o   Religion or spirituality, if properly employed, encourages people to develop a sense of responsibility toward others and to be ethically disciplined.

Clearly, all of the views outlined here reflect aspects of emotional intelligence and are likely to enhance or contribute to relationship/marital stability and happiness.

INDEX

Patricia Covalt holds a Ph.D. in clinical psychology and has been a psychotherapist in private practice since 1980. She specializes in several areas, one of which is committed adult relationships and marriage. As a Licensed Marriage and Family Therapist, Dr Covalt has treated hundreds of couples in clinical and workshop settings. She also provides supervision and mentoring to students and clinicians seeking further credentialing.

This author's professional experience includes extensive college and university teaching, public speaking, and workshop facilitation.

She established and operates a retreat center in the Colorado Rockies where she facilitates workshops and weekend retreats in this serene and remote setting. The author holds a membership in the American Psychological Association and serves on the Board of the Rocky Mountain Trauma and Dissociation Society. She is a clinical member of the American Association of Marriage and Family Therapy and serves as Chair of the Speakers Bureau for the Colorado Association of Marriage and Family Therapy.

Dr. Covalt is the mother of two adult daughters, each engaged in pursuit of careers in helping professions. As a person of high energy and contagious optimism, she maintains an active lifestyle of bicycling, hiking, skiing, and traveling with her companion of seven years, an aerospace executive.